CAMBRIDGE MUSIC HANDBOOKS

Stravinsky: *Oedipus rex*

CAMBRIDGE MUSIC HANDBOOKS

GENERAL EDITOR Julian Rushton

Cambridge Music Handbooks provide accessible introductions to major musical works, written by the most informed commentators in the field.

With the concert-goer, performer and student in mind, the books present essential information on the historical and musical context, the composition, and the performance and reception history of each work, or group of works, as well as critical discussion of the music.

Other published titles

Stravinsky: *Oedipus rex*

Stephen Walsh

CAMBRIDGE
UNIVERSITY PRESS

Published by the Press Syndicate of the University of Cambridge
The Pitt Building, Trumpington Street, Cambridge CB2 1RP
40 West 20th Street, New York, NY 10011–4211, USA
10 Stamford Road, Oakleigh, Melbourne 3166, Australia

First published 1993

Printed in Great Britain at the University Press, Cambridge

A cataloguing in publication record for this book is available from the British Library

Library of Congress cataloguing in publication data
Walsh, Stephen
Stravinsky: *Oedipus rex* / Stephen Walsh
p. cm. – (Cambridge music handbooks)
Includes bibliographical references and index.
ISBN 0 521 40431 2 (hardback) – ISBN 0 521 40778 8 (paperback)
1. Stravinsky, Igor, 1882–1971. Oedipus rex.
I. Title. II. Series.
ML410.S00C00 1993
784.2'000–dc20 92–0000 CIP MN

ISBN 0 521 40431 2 hardback
ISBN 0 521 40778 8 paperback

AH

For Gaby, Beatrice,
Rupert and Richard

Contents

Preface

Since the present series of Music Handbooks is younger cousin to an earlier (and continuing) series devoted exclusively to opera, it may seem perverse to include in it a study of a work which most enthusiasts – starting with the composer himself – have regarded as an opera. There is a reason for this but no real excuse. The reason, quite simply, is my own opportunism, backed up by the publishers' tolerance. Invited to contribute to the Cambridge Music Handbooks, I suggested *Oedipus rex* knowing perfectly well that I could defend the choice on the grounds of the work's notorious generic ambiguity, even though I fully intended to prove beyond doubt that that ambiguity is a myth. It is true, of course, that *Oedipus* has often been given in concert form, ever since its Paris première on a theatre stage but with no production and no sets or costumes beyond black drapes and sombre garments. Today it is perhaps more often staged than in the past; but it still more than survives as a concert work, and for this reason – if for no other – I hope it will not be thought of me that 'scripsi quod nefastum est'.

Certainly, no excuse is needed for devoting a whole book to *Oedipus*. Of all Stravinsky's works outside the popular early ballets, it is perhaps the most widely admired and certainly one of the most frequently played. As a profoundly serious tragic masterpiece, it towers above all but a handful of other works (mostly by Stravinsky as well) composed in the feckless twenties. Moreover, it is a work with a story to tell: not only does it have an elaborate stylistic and generic history, but its own hybrid character sheds light on many aspects of early twentieth-century art, including theatrical production and design as well as literary and musical neo-classicism. Above all, it is a key work for Stravinsky himself. It is a living embodiment of many of his lifelong attitudes to style, form, expression, language, and the musical theatre; and as integrated drama, it can even be said to dramatise them – to the point where, behind their all too familiar masks of jargon and technicality, they gradually take on more general and appreciable significance. At least I hope that that is the case, and that non-specialist readers will not feel that here is just one more closed book for them.

I should like to thank the following friends and colleagues for their help: the staff of the Paul Sacher Stiftung in Basel and of the Music Department of the Library of Congress in Washington; my own music department at the University of Wales, College of Cardiff, who helped me with both time and money; Malcolm Smith of Boosey & Hawkes – always an unstinting fund of information on Stravinsky's publication history and related matters; Peter Dennis-Jones, who advised me on the Latin. Anthony Holden may or may not be surprised to learn that a number of my ideas – such as they are – on Stravinsky's *Oedipus* in its relation to Sophocles originated in conversations with him. As for my wife, perhaps, given the subject, her precise role is best left unspecified . . .

Oedipus rex is published by Boosey & Hawkes, who took over rights from the Edition Russe de Musique (the original publisher) after the war. Music examples are reproduced by kind permission, as are the English and Latin texts in Appendix A.

Abbreviations

Abbreviations are used in endnote references as follows (see Bibliography for publishing information):

Chron	Stravinsky, *Chronicle of my life*
Conv	Stravinsky and Craft, *Conversations with Igor Stravinsky*
Dial	Stravinsky and Craft, *Dialogues*
Expo	Stravinsky and Craft, *Expositions and Developments*
Poet	Stravinsky, *Poetics of Music*
SPD	Vera Stravinsky and Craft, *Stravinsky in Pictures and Documents*
SSC I, II, III	Craft, *Stravinsky: Selected Correspondence* (vols 1, 2 and 3)

1

The exile finds a new home

Like most very great artists, Stravinsky was by trade a synthesiser of experience. Works that seem to display the sublime detachment of pure art (whatever that may be) turn out to have complex origins in the social and intellectual life around him, origins which could hardly be guessed from the music but which, once known or suspected, can help us come to terms with complexities or even obscurities in the work itself.

There is nothing new about this; the nineteenth century offers several well-documented parallels (Schumann, Wagner, Mahler). All the same, the case of Stravinsky is in some respects unique. The Romantics thought of themselves as outcasts, but Stravinsky really was an outcast. Stranded in Switzerland when war broke out in 1914, he was finally cut off from his Russian homeland by the Bolshevik revolution of 1917, and thereafter he made only one trip to Russia, in 1962. He moved from Switzerland to France, then later (in 1939) to the USA, and materially speaking he settled wherever he lived: he was no spiritual outcast, like Mahler, nor consciously part of a diaspora, like Schoenberg. But quite simply he was detached from his cultural roots, something which has always made life hard for exiled Russian artists, whether they are like Chagall and resort to recurrent images of old Russia, or like Solzhenitsyn and more or less cease to work creatively.

For Stravinsky, exile meant grafting on to new creative roots, and it was at least partly a conscious process. The first signs appear already in the Three Easy Pieces for piano duet (1914–15), which are discreetly based on style parodies. But the first unmistakable product of the synthetic tendency was *The Soldier's Tale* (1918), where a mixture of Russianism, ragtime, popular marches, dances and a kind of Cubist chorale dramatises the story of the soldier for whom exile means the loss of his soul. Around 1920, the composer of *The Rite* was still able to draw on the pure springs of Russian musical ceremony. The *Symphonies of wind instruments*, a work which lacks overt synthetic features, was composed that summer, a year after the more or less totally synthetic *Pulcinella*, based on Pergolesi. But the days of this kind of Russianism were severely numbered, and by the time Stravinsky went to live

1

in Paris in September 1920 he was fast losing interest in the Russia of his teacher Rimsky-Korsakov: the Russia of fur hats and Orthodox chant and peasant weddings. In a letter published in *Le Figaro* in May 1922 before the premiere of his little Pushkin opera *Mavra*, he attacked the nationalism of the Five, and espoused instead the cosmopolitan tendency in nineteenth-century Russian music represented above all by Glinka and Tchaikovsky. *Mavra* itself is a trivial bourgeois farce, set in suburban St Petersburg and transparently using the idea of a culturally dehydrated milieu as a vehicle for a synthetic music which borrows idioms from here and there, just like the bourgeoisie itself.[1]

Mavra is a key work, less for its artistic merit (which is open to dispute) than for what it tells us about its composer's creative frame of mind at the time, and for what it led to in his later work. As a self-conscious style polemic, it candidly proclaims the advent of Stravinskian neo-classicism: that is, of a music in which style as such is part of the subject-matter. And it does so with the help of a supporting manifesto which – true to Parisian custom – attempts to justify the work historically, aesthetically and intellectually, in such a way as to identify those who disapprove as ignorant, tasteless and very probably stupid into the bargain. The *Figaro* letter was the first of a series of such manifestos, which Stravinsky or his assistant, Arthur Lourié, wrote to introduce his main twenties works, including *Oedipus rex*.[2] But while clearly eager to place himself in relation to the myriad fashions of his adopted home, he certainly was not anxious to drown his identity in that shallow but turbulent stream. The style models for *Mavra* are highly particular; they suggest that Stravinsky might be abandoning the Diaghilev-poster view of Russia, but was still asserting his Russianness. The models are studiously unfashionable, even while the posture of adopting them is *chic*. Glinka was virtually unknown in twenties Paris, and Tchaikovsky was hopelessly outmoded, a popular slushy romantic who wallowed in self-pity, when Jean Cocteau was busy telling Parisians that art had to be jolly and commonplace, trivial and witty.[3] Tchaikovsky was the last model one would expect an arch-modernist like Stravinsky to adopt. Yet, by the hallowed principle of *épater le bourgeois*, that was precisely where his most piquant modernism lay. The stylistic tease was, as we shall see, to become a hallmark of Stravinskian neo-classicism, and is a factor in *Oedipus rex*. *Mavra* suggests that it may well have originated at least partly in his *déraciné* state, and in the search for an idiom which would be both personal and novel, while capable of being related, more or less polemically, to certain general tendencies in French thought that were affecting the composer at the time.

We learn more about this from Stravinsky's next four works, all of them instrumental: the Octet (1922–3), Concerto for piano and wind (1923–4), Piano Sonata (1924) and Serenade in A for piano (1925). For four years he wrote nothing for voice, a medium which had previously preoccupied him for a whole decade. All the same, these instrumental works are in line with a noticeable orientation in his music since the start of the war: the move towards a drier, less resonant sound, with fewer instruments, an increasing emphasis on the harder kinds of wind sonority, on clattery instruments like the cimbalom, percussion in general, and eventually the piano, treated quasi-percussively and without the sumptuousness of romantic keyboard style. Though partly practical and economic, this tendency was at bottom aesthetic. At first Stravinsky seems to have been fascinated by the idea of squeaky peasant bands, while reacting sharply against the sound and fury and lumpish *art nouveau* rusticity of *The Rite*. Later his interest was drawn towards ragtime and jazz, just at the moment when popular culture was becoming intellectually fashionable in France as an antidote to the heavy self-communings of late romantic art and the misty fantasies of impressionism. 'The café-concert', Cocteau wrote, 'is often pure; the theatre always corrupt.'[4] By the time of his manifesto 'Some ideas about my Octuor', published soon after the premiere of the Octet in October 1923, Stravinsky seems distinctly under the influence of another remark of Cocteau's: 'Art is science made flesh. The musician lets number out of its cage, the draughtsman releases geometry.'[5] Before and during the early twenties, Stravinsky seems obsessed with everything cold and mechanical. He writes increasingly for the piano (even *Les Noces*, originally for a glorified peasant orchestra, settles for four pianos mediated only by percussion); he becomes hooked on the pianola, or mechanical piano, and starts arranging his music for it ('reconstituting it', he tells Satie).[6] Finally, in 'Some ideas about my Octuor', he presents a blamelessly constructivist interpretation of his recent work; he draws attention to its 'rigidity of form', its 'play of musical elements', its exclusion of all expressive nuance beyond what is provided by the counterpoint, instrumentation and tempo contrasts. Even the tone of the article is robotic, like that of Cocteau's Speaker in *Oedipus rex*, who 'expresses himself like a lecturer, telling the story in a detached voice'.[7]

Rappel à l'ordre

It is quite possible to see this phase of Stravinsky's work as a nervous response to cultural insecurity. But if so, it reflects not only his own uprootedness, but that of the time and place in which he was living. Cocteau's 'rappel à l'ordre' is only one expression of the contemporary mood. The need to restore order to art and society was felt even by those, like the poet Paul Valéry, who would never for a moment have been seduced by Cocteau's flippancies. Stravinsky's reading in the early twenties almost certainly included a little book called *Art et scolastique*[8] by the religious philosopher Jacques Maritain, who was at that time extricating himself from the soon-to-be-discredited right-wing Catholic movement Action Française and starting to promote a practical philosophy of life and art derived from the teachings of St Thomas Aquinas. Maritain's idea of art as a practical 'virtue', in which the artist takes on the aspect of a humble artisan striving to create work that will be as honest and well-executed as is within his power, was itself a clear reaction against the intellectual disorder of modernist tendencies in the Catholic Church. It was a kind of religious neo-classicism. From being a tortured hero obsessed with his own emotional malaise, the artist was to become a kind of ethereal watch-maker, who knows that if only his watch will keep time it will automatically be beautiful. Allowing for the didactic tone, this is very close to Stravinsky's message in nearly all his (and Lourié's) writings of the twenties and thirties, including the most important of them all, *The Poetics of Music*.

To what extent Stravinsky was directly interested in Maritain's religious ideas in the early twenties is hard to say for sure.[9] Though nominally a communicant of the Russian Orthodox Church, he had been brought up in an environment largely either passive (his parents) or antipathetic (his teacher Rimsky-Korsakov) towards religion. On his own later admission, he had not been to church since leaving Russia in 1910, though there is some evidence that he continued to be drawn to the ritual and iconography of the Orthodox church. After moving to Biarritz in 1921, the Stravinsky family had a confessor, and in Nice, from 1924, 'a certain Father Nicholas [Podossenov] . . . was practically a member of our household'.[10] Podossenov's precise role in Stravinsky's reconversion may emerge from a reading of his lengthy and numerous letters to the composer, as yet unpublished. What is already clear, however, is that at some time in 1925 such a reconversion took place, and that in April 1926 he returned formally to the Orthodox communion.[11] We do not know what prompted him. It may have been, as Craft suggests, a sense of guilt or emotional uncertainty surrounding his by then four-year-old affair with Vera Sudeikina, which he pursued in Paris and abroad, in the interstices of his conveniently provincial family life in the south of France.[12] It may have been affected by his wife's own growing religiosity under the threat of tuberculosis, a disease from which she suffered increasingly from 1914 until

4

her death from it in 1939. It may have been connected with a renewed creative need for richness and colour and hidden meanings, after the rather desiccated series of abstract instrumental works. More probably, all these things were no more than symptoms of a change not itself surprising or unusual in a man of forty-three, cast adrift from his own home and beginning to realise that he was unlikely ever to return there.

In September 1925, Stravinsky went to Venice to play his Piano Sonata in the ISCM Festival. He was suffering, he tells us in *Dialogues*, from 'a suppurating abscess in my right forefinger . . . I had prayed in a little church near Nice, before an old and "miraculous" icon, but I expected that the concert would have to be cancelled. My finger was still festering when I walked on to the stage . . . I sat down, removed the little bandage, felt that the pain had suddenly stopped, and discovered that the finger was – miraculously, it seemed to me – healed.'[13] On his way home from Italy, he stopped in Genoa and bought and read Joergensen's life of St Francis (in the French translation by Teodor de Wyzewa). 'To this reading I owe the formulation of an idea that had occurred to me often, though vaguely, since I had become *déraciné*. The idea was that a text for music might be endowed with a certain monumental character by translation backwards, so to speak, from a secular to a sacred language.'[14] The sacred language in St Francis's case was Provençal, which was literally his 'langue maternelle', since his mother was from Provence, though Francis was born and brought up in Assisi, spoke Italian as his first language, and according to Joergensen (quoting an unnamed earlier biography) knew 'French' (i.e. Provençal) only imperfectly.[15] Joergensen tells us that St Francis always begged for alms in 'French', and treated it as 'the language of his most solemn times'.

It may seem a far cry from this intimate character to the ostentatious monumentality of Jean Daniélou's Latin text in *Oedipus rex*.[16] But Stravinsky plainly needed no more than a hint to give substance to an already half-formed idea. As a Russian in process of renewing contact with his native church, he was as familiar as any Roman Catholic with the idea of a sacred language, since Russian Orthodox services are to this day conducted in Old Slavonic, a language almost as different from modern Russian as Latin is from Italian. Moreover, for the *déraciné*, the language of communication is at once a problem. Apart from his two early Verlaine songs (1910) and the Pergolesi arrangements in *Pulcinella*, Stravinsky had set no language but Russian to music, and it may well be that the growing predominance of instrumental works after 1918 was partly due to a reluctance to confide artistically in a language other than his own, while his own language was losing its creative immediacy for him, to say nothing of being quite incomprehensible to his audience.[17]

An opera in Latin

Soon after his return from Italy to Nice towards the end of September, Stravinsky wrote Cocteau a business letter confirming their collaboration on 'the idea which has pursued me for some time of composing an opera in Latin based on a universally known tragedy of the ancient world'.[18] The idea had been discussed in person a few days before, perhaps at a reading of Cocteau's new play *Orphée* either in Nice or at the Hotel Welcome in Villefranche-sur-mer, a few miles away, where Cocteau lived for much of 1925 and 1926. Like Stravinsky, Cocteau had recently turned to religion, under the influence of Maritain, whom he met in 1924.[19] But his interest in classical theatre went some years further back. In 1922, he had made an abridged and modernised translation of Sophocles's *Antigone*, and, though there are no alienation devices there, it seems likely that the ideas of that kind in *Oedipus rex* were Cocteau's, including, certainly, the Speaker in his evening dress, a dim echo of the figure of Death in *Orphée*, who appears in a pink ball-gown and a fur coat 'in the very latest fashion'.[20] The language idea, however, was Stravinsky's. He insists, in his business letter, on 'my idea, which I guard jealously, of a musical work with a Latin text'. Perhaps the Speaker, who tells the story in the vernacular, was an author's compromise. Cocteau, whose classical work had consisted of translation and adaptation *into* French, can hardly have been enthralled at having to produce a text for translation *out of* that language. Stravinsky nevertheless showed him no mercy. He dismissed Cocteau's first draft (27 October) out of hand; and a second draft was apparently also rejected.[21] As late as 19 January 1926 Cocteau was writing to his mother complaining that 'for the third time he has obliged me to begin my work all over again', even though by this time Stravinsky was well advanced on the composition of the opening chorus.[22] Cocteau was also occupied in designing the piece for the stage, working partly with Stravinsky's eighteen-year-old son Théodore – though exactly how much Théodore contributed to the detailed draft scenario and décor which Cocteau drew up in March 1926 is hard to establish, in view of Cocteau's transparent wish to please the composer by praising Théodore and attributing certain strong ideas to him. The sketch tableau in the published score, for instance, is credited to Théodore, though the visual ideas it presents are unlikely to have been his.[23] As we shall see, the intention to stage the work survived almost into the very month of the first performance, and was finally abandoned only because of uncertain funding and shortage of time.

Writing the music

The actual composition of *Oedipus rex* and the negotiations over its first performance are unusually well documented, not least because of Stravinsky's restless life-style in the late twenties, which forced him to shelve the score no fewer than five times during the fourteen months it took him to compose it in draft, while at the same time ensuring that plans for the performance had to be communicated by letter. After working on the opening chorus for much of January 1926, he left Nice for Paris, returning at the end of the month to work on revisions to the score of *The Rite of Spring*. He then spent a fortnight or so with Cocteau presumably refining the stage conception, as reflected in Cocteau's draft of the following month. By 17 February, however, he was back in Paris, proceeding from there with Vera to Holland, where in Amsterdam on the 28th he conducted *The Rite of Spring* for the first time. In March he conducted in Budapest, Vienna, Zagreb and Milan, before returning to Nice (still, remarkably enough, with Vera) on the 26th.

For the next four or five weeks he worked on *Oedipus*, composing Creon's aria and much of Oedipus's 'Non reperias', before once again having to break off for an engagement in Milan, where he replaced Toscanini conducting *Petrushka* and *The Nightingale*, and perhaps saw Puccini's *Turandot*. After Milan he went to Paris with Vera, attending a rehearsal of Cocteau's *Orphée* in mid-June, then returning to Italy for further concerts in Milan and a two-week holiday with his wife Catherine. In July he was again in Paris, went to London to see *Les Noces*, then spent three more weeks in Paris (perhaps working in the Pleyel studio), and only returned to Nice (by car, still with Vera) on 3 August. Here he was able to work on *Oedipus* for several weeks, and by mid-September had completed the first part, and also Jocasta's aria up to the end of the first section (fig. 100). It was only at this stage that he decided to divide the work, adopting the repetition device from *Orphée* (the 'Gloria' with its repeat corresponds to the play's Scenes viii and viii*bis*). Then yet again he went to Paris for three weeks, apparently just to see Vera and to attend her house-warming party. Back in Nice, he completed Jocasta's aria, composed the duet 'Oracula mentiuntur', and much of the following scene with the Messenger and the Shepherd, before once more taking the train to Paris, where he may have discussed the question of finance for the work's premiere with the Princesse Edmond de Polignac. He left Paris with incipient flu on 18 December, but had recovered by the 28th, when he wrote to Ansermet that he was working 'comme 3 nègres'.[24] During January and early February 1927 he composed much of the rest of Act II, and began correcting proofs of the Act I vocal score, but, with the draft score still unfinished, broke off a fifth time to go to Paris, where he spent three weeks (including a brief trip to Nancy and Strasbourg). Not until 14 March did he at last complete the draft score, spending the rest of the month orchestrating the first act, and completing the scoring of Act II only on 11 May (appropriately enough in Paris), less than three weeks before the first performance.[25]

It seems to have been the authors' intention from an early stage to offer *Oedipus rex* to Diaghilev as a birthday present for the Ballets Russes to mark the company's twentieth season in 1927. There is no mention of this in Stravinsky's original business letter to Cocteau, but it is implicit in the secrecy surrounding the project, and becomes clear from Cocteau's letter of 19 January 1926 to his mother, where he notes his and Stravinsky's intention to help pay for the performance by taking part without fee. The difficulty about this, of course, was that, if the company was to perform the work, Diaghilev would have to be told about it in advance. Nevertheless he was still being fended off in February 1927, when Stravinsky wrote to Cocteau: 'I am stupefied by Diaghilev's behaviour . . . In questioning you about the subject of the work he gives the impression of knowing precisely that you are the one with whom I am collaborating – unless that was simply a provocation. I hope that you did not allow yourself to be taken in.'[26] Not until early April was Diaghilev openly involved, by which time it was becoming doubtful whether the work could be got ready in time for the Ballets Russes season in late May.

A macabre gift

Nor was there ever any doubt early on that the work would be staged. In his October 1925 letter, Stravinsky calls it an 'opera', and much of the ensuing correspondence with Cocteau is taken up with matters of décor. But by the time Diaghilev got wind of the project (and certainly by the time he knew about it officially), the 1927 season was planned and *Oedipus rex* became an extra work for which additional funds would have to be found. This difficulty is first mentioned in Cocteau's undated letter of about 20 December 1926. He has seen Mme de Polignac and discussed finance with her: 'the prospect of work and quarrels rejuvenates her and puts a sparkle in her eye'.[27] But Stravinsky was much less keen on this thought so long as composition was still in progress. Although he may have talked money on his Paris trip in February

1927 (there is a hint to this effect in his letter to Cocteau of 10 February, a week before he left Nice), he seems to have held aloof from any detailed involvement until the completion of the composition draft on 14 March, when he cabled Cocteau urging him to raise extra funds to pay 'the increased cost of singers'.[28] The problem was that the Princess had offered to back the performance, but was unwilling to release funds until the rest of the necessary money had been guaranteed, which naturally made it risky to enter into firm engagements with the musicians. With the draft score complete, Stravinsky pressed her to break this stalemate; but she did so only partially (in a letter, at once unctuous and evasive, of 20 March), in return for his promise to give an avant-première at her house. Meanwhile it was decided to approach the couturière Coco Chanel for the remaining guarantee. But Chanel played hard to get. Away from Paris when Cocteau first tried to contact her, she then made willing noises but at the crucial moment (on 7 April) left for a ten-day trip to Spain, carefully sidestepping a telegram from Stravinsky on the way.[29] By the time she returned (on the 17th) Stravinsky had lost patience and handed all the arrangements over to Diaghilev, who seems to have decided at once (and regardless of the extra money which Chanel made available on her return) that there was too little time to prepare a stage production.

This episode sheds a good deal of light on Parisian cultural politics in the twenties. Whereas in the past the patronage of art had flowed directly from centres of power, in the age of the common man it had become precisely a way of establishing power through money. It is no aspersion against the sewing-machine millionairess Mme de Polignac's excellent taste and genuine desire to promote the art she admired, to say that she was not above using the association with great art to manoeuvre for social influence. Cocteau, after at first defending her, eventually recognised her tactic of directing her own patronage towards the composer, leaving to Chanel the more expensive but less prestigious task of paying for the performance.[30] No doubt Chanel, herself a *commerçante* at first by no means well received in the Faubourg Saint-Honoré, saw the danger of being used in this way, responding first with delay, then with hauteur. Cocteau was eventually impressed: she 'took it very grandly', he told the composer, 'and was only interested in the work'.[31] Had he forgotten, or was he too carefully remembering, that Chanel had been Stravinsky's mistress when he first moved to Paris in the autumn of 1920? Throughout the *Oedipus* negotiations, Stravinsky treated her with caution, at first allaying Cocteau's suspicions about her intentions, then himself expressing doubts about them, while Cocteau became effusively pro-Chanel in his reports to Stravinsky on the progress of negotiations.[32]

The avant-première of *Oedipus rex* duly took place at a soirée at the Princess's house in Paris on 29 May 1927, with Stravinsky accompanying at the piano.[33] The official première, with orchestra, was the following night, in the Théâtre Sarah-Bernhardt, Stravinsky conducting. The concert performance of this austere masterpiece must have struck a sombre note on a programme consisting otherwise of ballets (probably Sauguet's *La Chatte* and Stravinsky's own *Firebird*), and it did not go down well either with Diaghilev's rather flighty clientèle or indeed with Diaghilev himself ('un cadeau très macabre', Stravinsky reported him as calling it).[34] But when it was staged, in Vienna and Berlin the following February, it hardly fared much better. In the next chapter, we shall examine the work's unusual treatment of its dramatic materials and its disconcerting mixture of theatrical conventions, which pose problems not often solved in performance, and which to this day challenge our sense of stylistic coherence and propriety.

2

Of masks, masses and magic

Anyone who has ever tried to follow the plot of Stravinsky's *Oedipus rex* intelligently with no prior knowledge of the story will know that it is in fact an impossible task. Even for the dwindling tribe of Latin scholars, there is little hope of understanding exactly why, for example, Oedipus takes so long to realise his true situation as King of Thebes, for the simple reason that in compiling the text Cocteau seems deliberately to have left out such vital information. These omissions are usually attributed to snobbery. Stravinsky himself came round to some such opinion: 'The line "And now you will hear the famous monologue, 'The Divine Iokaste is dead' ", is intolerable snobbery. Famous to whom? And no monologue follows, but only a four-word singing telegram.'[1] But the sketchy nature of Cocteau's dramaturgy is closely bound up with the whole theatrical genre of the work, with its conscious use of an arcane language, its statuesque stage idiom, its allusive, tableau-like format. In a tangible sense, *Oedipus rex* is not only about the fate of a king called Oedipus; it is also about the ways in which such a profound but apparently remote tale can be given meaning to modern audiences in the modern theatre. As such, it is by no means isolated, either in Stravinsky's work or in the theatre of his day. So before examining the opera-oratorio itself, it will be worth looking at its context in the work of Cocteau and others. But we should perhaps start at the very beginning, with the original Greek play by Sophocles, *Oedipus Tyrannus*.

The story of Oedipus was, in general terms, well known to fifth-century (BC) Athenians. There were accounts in the *Odyssey* and other epic poems of the Homeric period, as well as a play by Aeschylus, now lost. In watching Sophocles's play for the first time, therefore, most of the audience would from the start have known essential facts which, as a part of his technique of dramatic irony, Sophocles reveals only gradually to his *dramatis personae*.

They will have known that Oedipus was the son of King Laius of Thebes and his wife Jocasta; that, because of an oracle which foretold that Laius would be killed by his own son, the child had been exposed on a mountainside but

11

rescued by a kindly shepherd of the Corinthian king Polybus, taken to Corinth and brought up as Polybus's adopted son. One day, Oedipus was teased by a friend for not resembling his parents. Anxious to find out the truth, he consulted the oracle at Delphi and, learning that he was fated to kill his father and marry his mother, he decided not to return to Corinth but made his way towards nearby Thebes. On the way, where the road forks between Delphi and Daulis, he was roughly handled by the servants of an old man in a chariot, and in retaliation killed them all (except for one servant), unaware that the old man was King Laius on his way to consult the oracle about the Sphinx which was ravaging Thebes. Oedipus continued on to Thebes, where he himself encountered the monster, solved its riddle and drove it to suicide. The Thebans naturally received him as a saviour, made him their king and gave him Laius's widow Jocasta as his wife. But the gods sent Thebes a plague; and when Jocasta's brother Creon consulted the oracle, he learnt that the plague was a punishment for harbouring Laius's murderer. In the play, Oedipus, the solver of riddles, sets himself to find the murderer. He soon begins to realise that he himself is the man; but it is only when a Messenger arrives with news of Polybus's death that the story gradually comes out of the circumstances of Oedipus's adoption, and Oedipus is forced to recognise that the man he killed was his own father and the woman he married his own mother.

Cocteau's cocktail

The account of this story given in the vernacular by Cocteau's Speaker is defective in many crucial respects. It mentions Oedipus's reluctance to return to Corinth, without ever explaining that it is because he still regards Polybus as the father he is fated to kill. But without this vital information (and its geography of attendant facts) the whole resolution of the drama is inexplicable, since once Oedipus begins to suspect he is Laius's murderer it is hard to understand why he does not there and then see that he has committed the very parricide and incest predicted by the oracle. Sometimes, on the other hand, Cocteau gives necessary information confusingly. For instance, the Speaker says that it is Oedipus's accusation of collusion with Creon that decides the blind seer Tiresias to reveal the royal identity of Laius's murderer. But in the Latin text of the opera-oratorio (as in Sophocles) Oedipus first accuses Tiresias of the murder, and only then, after Tiresias has angrily revealed the oracle, suggests a plot against his throne. Sophocles is careful to tell us additionally that it is Creon who has suggested consulting Tiresias, whereas Cocteau gives no hint of this important motive for Oedipus's suspicion of a plot.

Why should Cocteau muddle things in these ways? Obviously the spoken narration had to be succinct, and it had to include Oedipus's accusation of Creon because it is their consequent row which attracts Jocasta's attention and motivates her speech about the 'trivium'. So the accusation against Tiresias had to go, and the order of events be changed to keep 'le roi est un roi' ('the king is a king') as the overlapping cue for the chorus entry. Yet after all this, Cocteau actually leaves out the 'dispute of the princes', which the Speaker gives as the reason for Jocasta's intervention. Creon in fact never reappears after Tiresias's monologue. So the poor audience remains blissfully ignorant of Oedipus's wild accusations against his brother-in-law, which – in Sophocles – are what prompt Jocasta's well-meaning revelation about the road junction. A final confusion comes in the next section, where, according to the Speaker, 'the witness to the murder emerges from the shadows. A messenger announces to Oedipus the death of Polybus . . .'. The clear implication is that the witness and the messenger are one and the same. But this is not the case. In fact the only witness of the murder in Sophocles is the shepherd, who had been the sole survivor of Laius's retinue but who, when he knew that Oedipus was in Thebes, had begged to be sent far from the city. This shepherd is, indeed, named as a witness in Cocteau's Latin text, though one would need sharp ears as well as excellent Latin to catch the point, which flashes past during Oedipus's *tempo agitato* duet with Jocasta. Neither in the narration nor in the Latin do we learn how the shepherd came to witness the murder.

In the frame

The real point of all this is surely that the 'narration' is actually not a narrative device at all, but a pseudo-narrative device: not outside the frame surrounding the stage-picture and the Latin text, but the actual frame itself. Cocteau saw that its articulative function was much more important than its story-telling role. And there is good reason to believe that at the time Stravinsky, for all his later disowning of the device ('that disturbing series of interruptions'[2]) thought so too, and played a full part in devising it.

Framing techniques of this kind are common in Stravinsky's earlier stage works. Already in *Petrushka* the nominal action is, literally, boxed up in the showman's booth, while the ballet spends more time describing the motley crowd going about its business and pleasure quite unaware of the miniature tragedy unfolding in its midst. Reality has many levels; and the theatre is uniquely equipped to play on our sense of what is real and what is artificial. Stravinsky must surely (though he never admitted it) have known about the work of the great Russian actor and producer Vsevolod Meyerhold, whose early experimental period coincided with Stravinsky's early adult years in St Petersburg. In December 1906, Meyerhold produced there Blok's symbolist play *Balaganchik* ('The Fairground Booth'), in which the central characters were those of the old *commedia dell'arte* and the stage was a small box-set which could be lifted bodily, in full view of the audience, into the flies. Between the set and the audience sat the 'Author', who could thus be observed creating the whole action and the machinery which set it in motion.[3]

Meyerhold later wrote a long and seminal article, named after Blok's play, setting out his ideas on stage production in the manner of the traditional travelling theatres, with their use of masks, dance, acrobatics and other devices long since relegated to the circus and the pantomime.[4] Meyerhold himself had worked in the realist theatre of Stanislavsky. But he soon rejected the idea of the 'theatre of four walls' and in its place evolved a concept of the theatre as a place where magic, artifice and the unforeseen can happen as a matter of course. Meyerhold cultivated a pantomime style based on 'the laws of the fairground booth, where entertainment always precedes instruction and where movement is prized more highly than words'.[5]

Most of Stravinsky's theatre works before *Oedipus rex* reflect these ideas. In particular *Renard*, with its re-creation of a rustic travelling theatre, and *The Soldier's Tale*, with its mixture of mime, dance and speech, its blend of fun and morality and its device of the Narrator figure who steps into and out of the action: these are purely Meyerholdian conceptions.[6] But the quasi-ritual action in *The Rite of Spring* and *Les Noces* also seems to reflect the symbolist idea of expression through stylised bodily gesture. It can be no coincidence that both Meyerhold and Stravinsky were lovers of puppet theatre, a medium in which facile realism is ruled out by the nature of the puppet itself 'with its incomparable movements, its expressive gestures achieved by some magic known to it alone, its angularity which reaches the heights of true plasticity'.[7]

One of the traditional roles of puppet theatre has been the presentation of well-known stories through a restricted repertoire of actions and gestures entirely familiar to the audience and expected by them as an integral part of the entertainment. The Punch and Judy show is the classic instance (Petrushka is a Russian equivalent). Historically these stories have their roots in the plays of the Italian *commedia dell'arte*, with their stock characters and more or less ritualised plots. It seems that the popularity of the *commedia*, as of other types of demotic theatre (including the medieval Mystery Play, not to mention the more recent Pantomime), lay precisely in the fact that people knew all the characters and usually knew what was going to happen to them.

The realist idea of drama as depending on the audience being kept in ignorance of the outcome has little relevance to these traditional plays, and it is certainly no accident that, at a time when writers and producers were turning against the realist theatre, they began to rediscover the *commedia* and to include its stock characters among their *dramatis personae*. *Petrushka* is admittedly a somewhat hybrid example, since the hero finally abandons his booth and, in the very act of dying, craves admission to the 'real' world of the fairground itself. But Stravinsky's subsequent theatre pieces nearly all adopt a ritualised action in which the idea of 're-enactment' is part of the implied relationship between the audience and the stage, whether they are watching stock plays, as in *Renard* or *Pulcinella*, or eavesdropping on some remote seasonal festival, as in *The Rite of Spring* or *Les Noces*, or watching a marionette play in the guise of a deliberately desiccated bourgeois satire played by flesh-and-blood singers, as in *Mavra*.

A static theatre

The grandest example of ritualised theatre that has come down to us is the Greek drama of Aeschylus, Sophocles and Euripides. As early as 1907, Meyerhold wrote that 'the Greek classical theatre is the very theatre which modern drama needs: it has three-dimensional space, no scenery, and it demands statuesque plasticity'.[8] 'The need,' he wrote in another article of the same period, 'is for a static theatre . . . the greatest of the classical tragedies . . . are all "static" tragedies.'

Tragedy in which there is no action in the exposition of the plot, and which is based on the interrelation of Fate and Man, requires a static theatre with a technique embodying movement as plastic music, as the external depiction of an inner experience (illustrative movement), so that restrained gestures and economy of movement are preferable to the gestures of public declamation. This technique shuns all superfluous movement, lest it distract the spectator's attention from the complex inner emotions conveyed by a rustle, a pause, a break in the voice, or a tear which clouds the eye of the actor.[9]

This is suggestively close, in both concept and terminology, to Stravinsky's description more than fifty years later of the theatrical motivation behind his *Oedipus rex*:

I consider this static representation a more vital way to focus the tragedy not on Oedipus himself and the other individuals, but on the 'fatal development' that, for me, is the meaning of the play . . . My audience is not indifferent to the fate of the person, but I think it far more concerned with the person of the fate and the delineation of it which

15

can be achieved uniquely in music . . . the portrait of the individual as the victim of circumstances is made far more starkly effective by this static presentation.[10]

Meyerhold hints at a psychological reading of the kind that Stravinsky explicitly rejects. But in terms of the stage picture, the kinship is obvious.

Although this kind of evidence supports Stravinsky's claim that the underlying theatrical concept of *Oedipus rex* was his own rather than Cocteau's, his sudden enthusiasm in the mid-twenties for an operatic version of Sophocles almost certainly did not come from a reading of Meyerhold or the direct experience of his work in the theatre. *The Fairground Booth* did, it seems, reach Paris in 1923, but in a production by the actor Georges Pitoëff, and in any case there is no evidence that Stravinsky saw it. What he almost certainly had seen at the time that he was planning *Oedipus rex* was two adaptations by Cocteau: his updated translation of Sophocles's *Antigone*, which opened in Paris on 20 December 1922, and his tragedy *Orphée*, of which Stravinsky heard a reading in late September or early October 1925 and probably attended a rehearsal in Paris on 15 June 1926, two days before the premiere.[11]

The boulevardier as tragedian

These Cocteau plays are utterly different one from another; but they add up to a specific and important tendency in the Parisian theatre of the twenties, and one which plainly influenced Stravinsky, however much he may later have tried to play down Cocteau's contribution to *Oedipus* itself. On the one hand they reflect a specifically Gallic desire (already apparent in the pre-war music of Debussy and Ravel) to reject the swooning and overpowering ecstasies of late romantic art, and seek stability in the Attic dignity of classical tragedy. *Antigone*, which is really a cut-down, deflated, but essentially faithful, speech-for-speech prose translation of Sophocles, shows that even the Greeks were to be denied any opportunity to rant. But there is no sign yet of the chic, boulevardier elements that make *Orphée*, and to a lesser extent *La Machine infernale*, such a striking expression of Cocteau's belief − well-known to readers of his musical manifesto *Le Coq et l'arlequin* (1918) − that art should be fun. One hardly knows whether to laugh or cry when, in *Orphée*, Death appears as 'a young and very beautiful girl in a bright pink ball gown and a fur cloak', or when Eurydice dies after licking a poisoned envelope, or when the Head of Orpheus, interrogated by a music-hall police inspector, gives its name as Jean Cocteau ('what an outlandish name', sneers the policeman). But although Cocteau's first draft libretto for *Oedipus rex*, which seems to be more or less the text he published as an independent play in 1928, is much closer in approach to *Antigone*, it may well have been the example of *Orphée* which triggered off the multi-level style-acrobatics of Stravinsky's music. The composer later used the Dada expression 'Merzbild' (a picture made from rubbish) to describe this aspect of *Oedipus*. But he overlooked the fact that his banalities are far from the gratuitous collisions of unrelated images that are the essence of Dada and, to some extent, the later Surrealism. Cocteau was despised by the Surrealists Breton, Picabia and the rest for (among other more circumstantial reasons) his lack of commitment to a truly radical art: *Orphée* remains, with all its bizarreries, a myth turned into a drawing-room conversation piece. And *Oedipus rex*, too, was to suffer at the hands of those who saw Stravinsky's espousal of a quasi-popular neo-classicism as a betrayal of the modernism to which he and his admirers had once laid claim.

Cocteau's published play *Oedipe-Roi* is dated 27 October 1925, that is just over a fortnight after Stravinsky's formal letter setting out the operatic project and establishing the terms of the collaboration.[12] Like *Antigone*, it takes the form of a cut-down prose translation of Sophocles's play, which it follows closely and in detail. Stravinsky later described it as 'precisely what I did not want: a music drama in meretricious prose'.[13] But what he seems to mean is that it was a prose text which invited a through-composed setting in the post-Wagnerian manner, whereas he had asked for 'a conventional libretto with arias and recitatives'. This kind of formal artifice, though an essential ingredient in Stravinsky since *Pulcinella* and *Mavra*, is lacking in Cocteau's earlier plays, and it seems to have given him some trouble. There is nothing of the kind in the first draft, unless one counts the Prologue, very much longer than the opening narration in the opera-oratorio, but recognisably parent to it, with its exhortatory opening 'Spectateurs!' and its 'Sans le savoir, Oedipe est aux prises avec les forces qui nous surveillent de l'autre côté de la mort', mixed into a rather lengthy, anecdotal story-so-far. Apart from the Prologue, there is no narration, or at least none surviving in the published version, though Cocteau may well have already intended some such device, knowing that his text was to be sung in Latin. At any rate the Speaker was an integral part of the libretto by, at the latest, mid-January 1926, when Cocteau wrote to his mother that 'I shall be the speaker who tells the story of each scene'.[14] Since he had meanwhile had to rewrite the libretto twice, at least in part, to satisfy Stravinsky's formal requirements, it is natural to see the Speaker less as a comprehension aid than as a structural device both for articulating the musical *tableaux vivants* of the Latin setting and for emphasising their monumentality and artificiality. This is certainly its artistic effect, as we shall see in the next chapter. But we do not, in actual fact, know exactly how it arose. We know only that Stravinsky, who had approved the dinner-jacketed Narrator in *The Soldier's Tale*,[15] came to detest its use in *Oedipus rex*, and even in the fifties sometimes performed the work without it, though he finally had to admit that 'alas, the music was composed with the speeches and is paced by them'.[16]

One senses in all this a certain tension between the different sources of Stravinsky's inspiration. Meyerhold's idea of a statuesque, tableau-style treatment of Sophocles certainly would not have precluded stylistic collisions of the Cocteau type. But nor does it instantly suggest the modish boulevardier quips by which the author of *Orphée* may well have felt tempted.

A chorus without a face

Except possibly in *The Soldier's Tale*, with its intrusion of telephones and stock market reports into the fairytale world of Afanassiev, Stravinsky had always avoided anachronism within the frame of his stage works. In *Les Noces* or *Renard* or *Mavra* the interior world of the play is always self-consistent, however artificialised, while the irony, such as it is, is confined to the implied relationship between the audience and the re-created idiom of what they are watching/hearing. Only in *The Soldier's Tale* is this relationship mediated, by a Narrator who, though initially outside the frame directing our attention into it, sometimes himself steps into the story and gives the soldier advice. It is no coincidence that this score marks the first appearance in a Stravinsky stage work of that stylistic self-consciousness that led in due course to neo-classicism. Style has become an issue in the story of a soldier who tries to enjoy the past, the present and the future all at once, and is punished for it. By the time of *Mavra* and the instrumental works that followed, style and genre were firmly established as subject matter. And it is fairly clear from Stravinsky's early ideas for *Oedipus rex* that the relation between the viewer and the viewed, the hearer and the heard, was the strongest initial impression here as well. The Latin text would confer a certain monumentality, as if the audience were like a party of tourists at Delphi or the Acropolis, knowing the history of those sites but separated from a direct experience of their meaning by a distance of culture and language. But this gap would not be bridged by anachronism. Perhaps it would not be bridged at all: there is at first no mention of a Speaker. And when he does appear, the Speaker assumes something of the drama's own monumentality. He speaks to us in our own language, but since he does not tell us what we need to know it may be that he is not speaking to us at all but to some other audience, as monumental as himself: an audience invisible but symbolically present – a kind of ideal tourist party, turned to stone just outside the margins of the stage picture.

To Meyerhold, with his interest in the theatre as a fluid and liberated medium, this might well have seemed a rigid concept. But it is consistent with his idea of a statuesque Greek drama. Moreover, Stravinsky's underlying stage picture has a strongly Meyerholdian ring. 'I saw the chorus first', he says in *Dialogues* (p. 23), 'seated in a single row across the stage . . . I thought that the singers would seem to read from scrolls, and that only these scrolls and the outlines of their bearers' cowled heads should be seen. My first and strongest conviction was that the chorus should not have a face.' From here it was a short step to the use of masks. The preface to the score presents a refined stage of this conception. 'Except for Tiresias, the Shepherd and the Messenger, the characters remain in their built-up costumes and in their masks. Only their arms and heads move.' These box-like costumes are reminiscent of Meyerhold's original setting for *The Fairground Booth*, which includes 'figures . . . cut out of *cardboard* with frock-coats, shirt-fronts, collars and cuffs drawn on with soot and chalk. The actors' hands are thrust through openings in the cardboard torsos, and their heads simply rest on the cardboard collars.'[17] A letter of about 20 January 1926 from Cocteau to Stravinsky suggests that the librettist may have come up with this idea for *Oedipus*. 'I have found the trick [truc]', he writes, 'and finished all of the . . . masses . . . boxes.'[18] He had probably been researching solutions to problems that had come up in discussion with the composer, perhaps even as a result of Stravinsky's criticisms of the first draft text.

Vanishing tricks

Yet whether Cocteau was contributing or merely executing, there are striking similarities between these various devices and certain mechanisms in his own *Orphée*, which Stravinsky had heard but not yet seen. The printed text of *Orphée* includes a suggested décor very like the one in the published score of *Oedipus rex*, even down to the fixed figure of the horse, and the mirror through which Death makes her entrances and exits, in exactly the same position (stage left) as the grotto in *Oedipus* which opens to reveal the 'fountain of truth', Tiresias. The stylisation of entrances and exits is a central consideration in the preface to *Orphée*, just as it is in Stravinsky's ideas for *Oedipus*. 'My first conception', he tells us, 'was that the people of the play should be revealed from behind small individual curtains, but I realized later that the same effect might be accomplished more easily by lighting.'[19] One wonders how much later. In *Orphée* Eurydice's disappearance, when Orpheus looks back at her, is achieved slowly through an elaborate trick of lighting, which Cocteau insists on even in theatres with trapdoors. But in Cocteau's notes of March 1926 for *Oedipus* the only comparable use of lighting accompanies the appearance of Tiresias, at which the stage lights dim and the seer is picked out by a spotlight, exactly like the head of Orpheus when it is thrown on to the stage in the play. But even the preface in the score adds nothing more on lighting. Indeed 'the disappearance and reappearance of Oedipus in the Second Act takes place slowly, on the spot and by means of a trapdoor, as in a fairy scene', a procedure which resembles Cocteau's instruction about Eurydice in every respect *except* the crucial one of lighting.

According to one editor of Cocteau's play, '*Orphée* is unique in the modern French theatre in being published complete with such detailed set designs and descriptions of costumes',[20] which makes it the more probable that much of the detail of the *mise en scène* of *Oedipus rex* originated either directly with Cocteau or through contact with his recent work. It may however be observed that the first *Orphée*, in June 1926, was directed by Georges Pitoëff, who had, as we saw earlier, worked on *The Fairground Booth* as recently as 1923. Pitoëff, a Georgian actor-director who, like Meyerhold, had worked with Stanislavsky in St Petersburg, was certainly acquainted with Meyerhold's work, having come to Switzerland from Russia only in 1915. Pitoëff believed in a kind of pure textuality, in which austerely planned abstract sets encouraged 'the plastic translation of the work's secret poetry',[21] but he also believed in theatre as a place where the illusory and provisional character of modern life found its ideal expression. His productions of Pirandello in the early twenties were among the first in Paris. But he also worked on the Paris production of *The Soldier's Tale* (1924).[22] So there are complex threads linking Stravinsky and Cocteau to pre-war Russian symbolism by way of the modern French theatre.

But whatever the exact theatrical parentage of *Oedipus rex*, it differs sharply from *Orphée* – and from much of Cocteau's other work in the theatre and cinema – in the relative unimportance of the techniques of illusion and artifice set out in its preface. Illusion is part of the fabric of *Orphée*, and the play is hard to imagine without it. In *Oedipus*, by contrast, illusion is necessary, at most, only insofar as the statuesque presentation may be deemed to preclude conventional stage movement, entrances, exits and so forth. Even then, the work's austerity can readily encompass a style in which the characters remain on-stage throughout, and simply step forward – or are spotlit – when they participate in the action. This is consistent with Stravinsky's original idea, in which 'I did not even allow them exits and entrances'.[23] And it brings us for the first time to the question of genre raised by the work's hybrid subtitle, 'opera-oratorio'.

Enter the composer

Stravinsky's account, in *Dialogues*, of the origins of *Oedipus rex* suggests that he thought of it, from the first, as a static stage picture. It was normal with him to start out from such mental images, like the famous 'waking vision' of *The Rite of Spring*, or the account, also in *Dialogues* (p. 39), of the dream that gave him the ensemble for the Octet. But these are, in the end, mere anecdotes, whereas the description of *Oedipus* is generic. The drama would be static, a 'still life' (as the composer recalls having told Cocteau); the central characters would remain rigid, moving 'only their heads and arms . . . like living statues',[24] but restrained even in such movements, not turning to listen to each other, and masked so that facial expression would be precluded. The stage itself was to be one-dimensional, with 'all the action [taking] place in the foreground'.[25] It sounds like a description of Japanese Kabuki or Noh, as filtered through the symbolist theatre of Maeterlinck, Meyerhold and the Surrealists; and no doubt these were all active influences on the theatrically highly literate Stravinsky's thinking. But one other important impulse remains to be taken into account: for Stravinsky the determining one of music.

Oedipus rex followed a fairly long period of purely instrumental, non-theatrical composition; after *Mavra*, as we saw in the last chapter, he had written a wind octet, and a concerto, a sonata and a serenade for piano (as well as completing the instrumentation of *Les Noces* and making various arrangements of his own music, including the Suite no. 1 for orchestra). To some extent this preoccupation with instrumental writing was circumstantial. Stravinsky's name still figured prominently, and with apparently new work, on the theatrical billboards of the early twenties;[26] but the only really new score in all this, *Mavra*, was a failure, and the composer was already turning to the piano (and the pianola) as a means of making that living with which, for all his fame, the theatre had so signally failed to provide him.

The concerto, sonata and serenade were all written for his own use. But they had also an aesthetic motive. One attraction of the piano as a creative medium at this time (rather than merely as a creative tool, which it had always been and always remained for Stravinsky) was that its hard, crystalline, percussive sound had come to embody certain artistic tendencies that attracted him after the First World War: the idea of a purely 'objective' kind of music, stripped bare of romantic sentiment and gush, rational, at times even mechanical, and always strictly under the composer's control. Such ideas are explicit in the manifesto Stravinsky published in 1924 after the first performance of his Octet, 'Some ideas about my Octuor'.[27] Here we read for the first time about the expressive role of form and counterpoint – of those complex elements, in other words, that remain firmly the purview of the composer. As for those nuances which the performer habitually assumes as part of his 'interpretation', Stravinsky denies that any are needed beyond the implicit terracings and bald dynamic contrasts given in the score. Since the form is controlled by a carefully planned scheme of tempo and textural contrasts, it follows that the performer has only to do what the score tells him in order to realise the composer's expressive intentions, as embodied in the form.

The similarity between this image of musical performance and Stravinsky's account of the stage picture in *Oedipus rex* is extremely striking. In both cases, the performer is supposed to subdue all personal desire for expression, all idiosyncrasy, all individuality of gesture, and instead become as nearly a statue as is consistent with the physical performance of his part. The instrumentalist, like the operatic singer, puts on a mask provided for him by the composer. And the singer, in order to avert the danger of superfluous expression through words, sings in Latin, 'the dead, desiccated language of chemists and lawyers', as Stravinsky's assistant, Arthur Lourié, described it.[28]

So it looks as if the theatrical form of *Oedipus rex* is as much a reflection of its composer's musical development in the decade after the First World War, as it is a response to the theatre of Cocteau or the symbolists. And its classicism is an issue as much of musical aesthetics as of narrative subject-matter or *mise en scène*. So it is high time to consider the music.

3

In which the music unfolds

Like most pigeon-holes in music history, the term 'neo-classicism' collects a lot of mail for quite different addressees. What looked at first like a bachelor flat turns out to be what T. S. Eliot's Prufrock would have called a one-night cheap hotel, where the clientèle is numerous, mobile, and often pseudonymous. The streets lead us to the overwhelming question that we cannot, unlike Prufrock, avoid asking: What is it?

For a start we can answer that it is, comprehensively, a misnomer. What the great aesthetic postmaster seems to mean by 'neo-classicism' is neither new ('neo') nor classical; or rather its classical elements are not new, and its new elements are not classical. There is new classicism all around us in music: in Berlioz, Mendelssohn, Tchaikovsky, Brahms – but also in Palestrina, Bach, Beethoven, Schoenberg and Panufnik. But it is not – or only rarely – 'neo-classical'. These composers are, of course – by one of those delightfully Chestertonian confusions of the English language – classics, and their music is, by another such confusion, classical (in the sense that, for some reason, Irving Berlin's, Elvis Presley's and Miles Davis's is not). But its 'classicism', such as it is, has nothing to do with either attribute. It consists in an unconscious or semi-conscious desire on the part of the composer to 'classicise' his writing: to reject extravagance and obfuscation in favour of clarity, balance, restraint and a strict formal economy. This tendency is part of the regular cycle of action and reaction in the history of all forms of expression. After the night's debauch, we drink cool, clear water and try to forget. But though neo-classicism may and frequently does include such things, they are not its most salient feature. The innocent-looking prefix brings with it a whole cargo of extra meaning which crushes any normal sense of the term it modifies.

In art, neo-classicism is a pre-twentieth-century idea. But even in its sixteenth- and eighteenth-century guises it was already self-conscious: a classicism for classicism's sake, a *revived* classicism. The sense of restoring antique values that have somehow been lost or perverted is fundamental both to the Renaissance and to the Greek revival of two and a half centuries later.

At the time this was regarded as perfectly natural – a simple process of restoring order and seriousness to art – and only much later was the term 'neo-classical' itself coined as a pejorative description of a kind of eighteenth-century art that the later Romantics regarded as insipid and artificial. The term recognised a tension between the classicising tendency in the art itself and the stiff formalism which, in the later view, undermined its claim to be regarded as a true and spontaneous expression. The 'neo', in other words, stood for a repertoire of critical aspersions: 'academic', 'cold', 'formal', 'unnatural' (in the Romantic sense), 'artificial'.

When it attached itself to modern music in the 1920s, the term absorbed this tension of meanings into a more complex pattern of historical and aesthetic allusion. No longer was it a simple question of critic versus artist, or one age versus another. Stravinsky himself, writing in 1923 at the time of his Octet, claimed as merits of his latest work precisely that formalism and that objectivity which nineteenth-century critics had rejected in the work of painters like David.[1] Admittedly he does not refer to his music as either classical or neo-classical. But still the idea of a restored classical 'virtue' is so blatant that it is no surprise to find it emerging explicitly in the writings of Arthur Lourié during the next four or five years. Yet Lourié is ambivalent, to put it mildly, about the exact force of this neo-classicism. He first brings it up as a property of Beethoven's late piano sonatas, which he sees as representing the struggle between individualism and 'the basic principles of sound itself . . . Just like [he goes on] the struggle in ancient tragedy between the hero and the chorus'.[2] Later, in a seminal article on the opposition between Stravinsky and Schoenberg, Lourié refers openly to 'the neo-classical music launched by [Stravinsky]', though he also makes it clear that neo-classicism itself has degenerated into 'the wholesale imitation and production of old and outworn formulas, . . . a technical process stamped with the mark of facile eclecticism', while Stravinsky himself 'is no longer even a neo-classicist'.[3] Lourié was writing less than a year after the first performance of *Oedipus rex*, and no doubt he was thinking particularly of that work as he tried to free the composer from the terminological noose into which he had put his neck. For *Oedipus* makes short work of such simple-minded definitions, and to form a better idea of the true nature of its revivalism, we have to go farther back in Stravinsky's work than the Octet.

Models and objects

As we saw in chapter 1, 'Some ideas about my Octuor' was not his first contribution to that peculiarly French genre, the artistic manifesto. In May

1922, at the time of the première of *Mavra*, he wrote an open letter to *Le Figaro* praising Glinka, Dargomizhsky and Tchaikovsky at the expense of the Russian Nationalists with whom he had previously, and rightly, been connected in people's minds.[4] The letter was a frankly polemical gesture. *Mavra* itself was a conscious attempt at a sophisticated neo-Russianism with its roots, not in the picturesque ethnographic tradition of Mussorgsky and Rimsky-Korsakov on which his own earlier music had drawn, but in the more urbane western-influenced work of Pushkin, Glinka and Tchaikovsky (to whose collective memory *Mavra* is dedicated). The text itself is based on Pushkin, and the music is self-consciously modelled on Glinka and Tchaikovsky.

Mavra may not be one of Stravinsky's best works, but it is one of his most self-revealing. It suggests that in 1921 he was thinking hard about what it meant to be a Russian exile in western Europe. It also shows that, whether or not for this reason, he was being drawn towards what might be called Apollonian models: models in which form and method take precedence over raw expressive individuality.[5] Above all, it shows an already well-developed tendency to treat such models as a source not just of inspiration but of actual musical material. Strictly speaking, Stravinsky had been 'borrowing' material in this way for more than a decade. *Petrushka* is to a significant extent based on musical found objects (Russian folk tunes and town cries, Viennese waltzes, French popular songs); and *The Soldier's Tale*, preceded and followed by various stylised piano marches, waltzes, polkas and ragtimes, uses the idea to dramatise a story about exile and the loss of spiritual identity. But these allusions had not yet fully penetrated Stravinsky's own style, as is evident from the *Symphonies of wind instruments*, which – written in 1920, and a fully characteristic masterpiece – shows no trace of them. In this sense *Mavra* is the turning-point. It anticipates many details of style and technique often specifically associated with neo-classical works like the Octet or the Concerto for piano and wind. Yet its own musical allusions are not, in any normal meaning of the word, classical. What it seems to establish is the *idea* of a style-based formalism. But its answer to the question of what that style should be is entirely provisional.

The instrumental works that follow not only answer the question but seem to make the classical association explicit. For one thing, they are abstract multi-movement pieces such as Stravinsky had not written since his student days, and they are plainly modelled – with however much licence – on 'book' classical forms: sonata, variations, rondo and so forth. In effect, formal classicism is grafted on to the existing idea of an allusive, or synthetic, style. At the same time 'classicism' (in the sense of Haydn or Beethoven) is, rather crudely it may seem, equated with 'form'. Stravinsky says things like: 'My

Octuor is a musical object [that] has a form and that form is influenced by the musical matter with which it is composed . . . .'[6] Such remarks could just as well have been made about the *Symphonies of wind instruments*; but it is part of the nature of things that they were not. The same is true of Stravinsky's notorious remarks about counterpoint and the 'play of movements [tempi] and volumes': for instance, 'Form, in my music, derives from counterpoint . . . the only means through which the attention of the composer is concentrated on purely musical questions.'[7] This observation is as meaningful, or meaningless, in relation to the Octet as it would have been in relation to the *Symphonies*. But it draws attention to the fact that one of the main allusions in the Octet is to the music of Bach, which stands as a reluctant foster parent to the kind of dry, mechanical, inexpressive music that was Stravinsky's answer to the uncertainties and insecurities of the immediately post-war years.

The preoccupation with form, objectivity, functionality and a certain clinical dryness and hardness was general in European art after the First World War. It was the ultimate cold douche after (as everyone then thought) the ultimate debauch. But the question of stylistic dissociation is strictly speaking separate, and only became mixed up with the formal issue through the work of *déracinés* artists such as Stravinsky. The arrangement and pastiche of old music had been a commonplace in the nineteenth century (not only in France), and were used by Diaghilev as a convenient way of creating new work in an antique or exotic setting: Stravinsky's *Pulcinella* originated in this way. But Stravinsky's dance and ragtime parodies of the war years were indebted to a more recent French tradition of popular stylisations, of which the best examples were among the songs and piano pieces of Satie and Debussy. Such work goes with the urge to demythologise 'great' music, but it hardly impinges directly on such music, even when – as in *The Soldier's Tale* – it helps dramatise a lengthy folk tale. The idea that overt allusion to a formalised art might support a high-powered neo-formalism seems to be original with *Mavra*. And it is this idea that provides the key to Stravinsky's neo-classicism.

So, in the instrumental works that followed, the references to Bach, Beethoven and the rest are above all stylistic signals, cueing both the composer and the listener into the formalist mode. The formal modelling as such is extremely limited and usually deceptive. For instance, the Allegro first movement of the Octet opens with a slow introduction obviously meant to suggest Haydn or Beethoven, with its incisive dominant frame, its slightly pedantic use of contrary motion scales and melodic sequence, and its unexpected reversion to a text-book periodic phrase-structure, with regular (or quasi-regular) antecedents and consequents. These signals are so specific that one takes the ensuing sonata form for granted. But in fact it is nothing of the kind. The piece is tonal, sectional, and recapitulatory, certainly; but the form is A–B–C–B–A, and the C section is more baroque than classical, with running anapaestic figuration clearly derived from Bach's Brandenburg manner. The promiscuity of these references is not their least salient feature, and there is no reason to regard it as accidental. Stravinsky clearly wants us to identify his models in general terms, but only so as to tease us into an expectation which he can then deceive. Hence the finale's rapid switching between motor-baroque and jazz, by way of a trumpet tune worthy of a *thé dansant*. In fact these switches are an essential part of the style, since they effectively dehistoricise procedures that could otherwise fall back into the merely academic. They ensure that the music's formalism is perpetually called in question, and in the process intensified, by an informal associationism, rather as, in the paintings of Chirico or, a little later, Magritte, a surreal effect is achieved through an unconventional arrangement of highly stereotyped and sometimes photographically vivid objects. The Octet is thus tonal and periodic in the sense that Chirico is figurative (this is not meant to imply a direct equivalence between those attributes): that is, the grammar is suggested, disrupted, then replaced with a symbolic grammar similar to the original in general appearance and signification, but radically unlike it in its real, underlying meaning.[8]

It is against this background that we now turn to *Oedipus rex* itself.

The German general

'As soon as my *Sérénade* was finished,' Stravinsky tells us in his autobiography,

I felt the necessity for undertaking something big. I had in mind an opera or an oratorio on some universally familiar subject. My idea was that in that way I could concentrate the whole attention of the audience, undistracted by the story, on the music itself, which would thus become both word and action.[9]

Hitherto he had written nothing remotely resembling an oratorio, and only two short operas: the immature and hybrid *The Nightingale*, and the tiny, featherweight *Mavra* – both somewhat untypical – while his most character-istic and successful work had nearly all been associated with ballet and mime. It seems obvious that the sudden impulse to compose a major choral work in an established genre grew out of his recent formal/synthetic tendency: 'oratorio' was to be the next stereotype after 'octet', 'piano concerto', 'sonata', 'serenade'. We may speculate (and the connection with Joergensen's *Saint*

Francis supports the idea) that his growing religious awareness, whatever its causes, helped push him in that particular direction. But Stravinsky remained pre-eminently a man of the theatre. He had been excited by Cocteau's *Antigone*, and, as we saw in the last chapter, he continued to envisage his most significant ideas as stage pictures. Moreover he had been working in the theatre, without the stimulus and satisfaction of major new creative work. *Renard* (1922), *Les Noces* (1923) and *The Soldier's Tale* (1924) were all old works which had had first or second performances in Paris since the composition of *Mavra*. There can never have been any serious doubt that, whatever its exact genre, the 'large-scale dramatic work' would be designed for the stage.

Its official model, none the less, turned out to be Handel: and not the Handel of the operas (which Stravinsky can hardly have known at that time, and which in any case do not typically have chorus parts), but the Handel of the oratorios, which are, precisely, dramatic works intended for statuesque (i.e. concert) presentation. There is a curious article by Lourié, written at the time of the first performance of *Oedipus rex*, which purports to describe Handel's role in the conception of Stravinsky's opera-oratorio.[10] Lourié describes the oratorio as an 'old form long dead . . . the exclusive preserve of conservatoire professors and no longer useful except as a competition test'. Handel, he suggests, was 'a German General of music [who] composed in London an impersonal music, as formal and conventional as legal language'.

If Stravinsky turns to Handel, it is not for reasons of taste or any individual sympathy for that composer, . . . [whose] music is tedious and suggests nothing so much as a coin worn out from passing through too many hands. But these formulae continue to possess a certain practical value. Stravinsky uses them in *Oedipus* as points of reference or compass-bearings, the contours thus established responding perfectly to the practical goals he sets himself in this particular case.

On the technical side, Lourié characterises Handel's music as 'statically harmonic', as compared with the 'dynamically polyphonic' Bach – the model for Stravinsky's previous neo-baroquisms. In *Oedipus rex*

harmonic dialectic . . . replaces polyphonic dialectic . . . The counterpoint is nearly always determined by the chord . . . it is not the harmony which flows from the counterpoint, as the traditional view has it, but on the contrary the counterpoint which is the consequence of the harmonies.

It is typical of Lourié's steely and bureaucratic style of argument that he appraises Stravinsky's music almost as unsmilingly as he does Handel's. In *Oedipus*, too, the polyphony articulates set harmonies, which are dictated and imposed on it in advance, just as children lay out their little bricks and put up buildings that follow the patterns they have in front of them.

Why anyone should bother their heads about such music, modelled so naively and mechanically on a despised and outworn tradition, is not clear.

Lourié's tone is that of the New Objectivity itself: cool, functional, clinical. It reflects, if not sympathetically, Stravinsky's own declared aims in *Oedipus*. But it is clearly too preoccupied with the formulae, not enough with the crucial role they played in stimulating the composer's imagination. 'In borrowing a form already established and consecrated,' Stravinsky pointed out a few years later,

the creative artist is not in the least restricting the manifestation of his personality. On the contrary, it is more detached, and stands out better when it moves within the definite limits of a convention. This it was that induced me to use the anodyne and impersonal formulas of a remote period and to apply them largely . . . . to the austere and solemn character to which they specially lent themselves.[11]

The first thing to be said about all this is that the historical Handel played no more than a symbolic role in the origins of *Oedipus*. Stravinsky was already thinking along 'impersonal' and 'objective' lines long before musical ideas began to form, as we know from his reasons for wanting to set a Latin text. In any case, the more one studies the supposed correspondences with Handel, the more they tend to disappear. Certainly *Oedipus* is (like Handel's oratorios) 'a large musical composition for soloists, chorus and orchestra, set to a serious and lofty text'.[12] Its apparently hybrid nature, as an opera-oratorio, recalls Handel's dramatic oratorios on classical subjects, like *Hercules* and *Semele* – works which have been successfully, if inauthentically, staged in modern times. But none of Handel's dramatic works are in Latin, and none of them are remotely like *Oedipus* in form or internal lay-out. Indeed the fluidity of the relation between soloists and chorus in *Oedipus* is closer in some respects to the Passion settings of Bach, though it is closer still to a much later model – the mature operas of Verdi. Handel's self-contained forms have no equivalent in Stravinsky. *Oedipus* comes closest to Handel in its monolithic choruses with their stereotyped imitative entries (rarely, in Stravinsky's case, extending as far as fugato, and never as far as fugue). But Stravinsky cannot, and seems not to want to, imitate the textural richness of Handel's choral writing, since he limits himself to male voices (perhaps in the interests of a Sophoclean stage-picture). Moreover there are no real recitatives in *Oedipus*, and few self-contained arias, though the aria set into a larger structure is certainly an important part of Stravinsky's scheme, as he warned Cocteau in advance.[13] There is some truth in Lourié's comparison of Stravinsky's harmony with that of Handel. But there is almost no stylistic resemblance. One does not feel (as one sometimes does in the Octet or the Concerto for piano and wind, and often in *The Rake's Progress*) any specifically eighteenth-century allusion. Only here and there in an aria is one put in mind of baroque music, and then usually for no more than a bar or two: Creon's aria, for instance, vaguely recalls, in this or that detail, a well-known Handel bass aria like 'Why do the nations'. But it is significant that, according to Stravinsky, it was complained after the first performance that 'la musique de Créon est une marche Meyerbeerienne'.[14]

It seems much more rewarding to think of *Oedipus rex* in terms of a complex set of symbolic allusions contrasted on a number of different levels. There is certainly evidence for some such synthetic view. Why would Stravinsky respond to an impulse to compose a large-scale theatre work to a Latin text with a quasi-Handelian setting of Sophocles? What is the significance of the blatant nineteenth-century Italianisms, to say nothing of what Stravinsky himself called the 'Folies Bergères' elements?[15] The answer surely is that the whole stylistic problem of *Oedipus rex* has been greatly exaggerated through the tendency to see it in its own monolithic terms as 'neo-Handelian', 'neo-Verdian' and so forth: in fact, as 'neo-classical' writ large. If instead the work were to be examined as an elaborate fusion of more or less discrete, more or less transparent musical and textual images, it might be possible to come closer to understanding the extraordinarily powerful and unified effect it actually makes, as a matter of common experience, in performance.

The Speaker as tour guide

According to the stage directions, the curtain rises directly on the chorus beseeching Oedipus to save Thebes from the plague ('Après le Prologue, rideau'). But this is not the first image in *Oedipus rex*. First we see and hear the Speaker, who enters in evening dress, speaks briefly ('like a lecturer' ('conférencier')), then exits: one imagines him moving in a brisk and business-like way. In French the word Speaker nowadays suggests rather a radio announcer or newsreader. But Cocteau's own recorded performances, though dry and monotonal, have the slightly heightened rhetorical pitch one might expect of a tour guide. And in just that spirit he announces the first part of the story with a certain deprecatory air, as though detailed explanations were unnecessary but a knowing sententiousness quite in order.

The real significance of the Speaker seems to be twofold. Technically, he articulates the drama into tableau-like sections whose framing in this way makes them to some extent inert and statuesque, since the action they depict follows a trajectory already implied (if not clearly narrated) by the Speaker. At the start, for instance, the Speaker's final two-word sentence, 'il promet' ('he promises': that is, Oedipus promises to save Thebes from the plague), is starkly juxtaposed with the violent protests of the chorus which are what, a few minutes afterwards, extract that promise. In later scenes the effect, as we shall see, is specifically and powerfully ironic.

More symbolically, the Speaker throws into relief both the complicated network of allusions in the music and dramaturgy, and the sheer monumentality of the drama. As a tour guide he satirises our voyeuristic condescension, our flippant air of having seen it all before, of 'doing' Sophocles today as we 'did' Shakespeare yesterday and shall 'do' Ibsen tomorrow: satirises it, because for all our god-like cultural superiority, we are moved by these masked, immobile figures in a way in which our own perhaps much worse fate seems unable to move us. As a master of ceremonies he authorises the work's diversity of style. As a newsreader he stands guard over these terrible events and reassures us that they are only moving pictures. He is, simply, modern man the voyeur, to whom all life is a newspaper or a TV picture or, now, a Visual Display Unit, and for whom pity is often not much more than a refined form of emotional masturbation. It is interesting that at this very period Piscator and Brecht were, in quite different contexts, adopting the narrative device of the news bulletin, using its dry factuality as an ironic frame for the most grotesque, violent and earth-shaking events. In *Oedipus rex* these qualities are ritualised; but they are there none the less, and it is the Speaker who focuses, characterises and perhaps in the end releases our response to them.[16]

As the curtain rises, the Speaker should exit; unlike the narrator in *The Soldier's Tale*, he is never a participant and should not intrude on the action. For the first scene, the curtain reveals Oedipus and the male chorus in position on stage; later, Creon appears, not by a conventional 'entrance' but by spotlighting or some other stage device (the preface in the score still suggests a curtain, though we know from *Dialogues*, p. 23, that this idea was superseded). Tiresias, similarly, is supposed to emerge semi-mechanically from behind a fountain (the 'fountain of truth'), stepping forward as the rock slides away. These are effectively the only characters in Act I.

The people and Oedipus

The first scene,[17] up to the second appearance of the Speaker, already encapsulates many of the work's most striking characteristics. The action is almost nil and the text brief, with much repetition, as in a baroque oratorio, but also as in much Italian opera. The chorus pleads with Oedipus to rescue Thebes from the plague; Oedipus, self-importantly, promises to do so and announces Creon's mission to the oracle. At the end, the chorus greets Creon himself in a paean of G major chords, *after* which the Speaker steps forward and introduces Oedipus's brother-in-law – a device Stravinsky uses again, with great dramatic force, for the entrance of Jocasta. But while the scene is dramaturgically for the greater part static, musically it is elaborate, discursive and to some extent evolving. It has a brief but forceful introduction, a long chorus in two parts (of which the second is quasi-fugal), a short but intense arioso for Oedipus, a varied reprise of the first part of the opening chorus, and Oedipus's final announcement, leading to the arrival of Creon. Moreover the musical imagery is both graphic and varied. The density is high, and, while denying his characters all facial expression and all but the most exiguous gesture, Stravinsky weaves a rich and complicated tapestry of musical allusion which is the real *locus* of the action.

The basis of this music, as Lourié was the first to point out,[18] is already to be found in Stravinsky's previous work, the piano Serenade in A. Here, in the first movement, we already find the smooth compound metre (6/8 bars alternating with 9/8) which typifies the opening *Oedipus* chorus, so different from the restless, irrational barrings for which Stravinsky was famous, and which still disrupt the 'classical' surface of the Piano Concerto. The harmony, too, is at bottom the same. It is a tonal (or what Lourié called 'tonic') harmony, with the third of the scale prominent, but the fifth either suppressed or atrophied and in any case no longer actively dominant in function. This 'tonality without fifths', as William E. Benjamin has called it,[19] is potentially somewhat inert, since it establishes centres without a criterion of movement away from them. But Stravinsky gets round the problem, in *Oedipus* at any rate, by accepting inertia as a specific dramatic property, by using it as the basis for sharp musico-dramatic images, and by varying inner voices contrapuntally, as he could more readily do in a choral than in a keyboard work. A comparison of the first main choral theme of the opera-oratorio with its obvious source in the first movement of the Serenade will help clarify the point (Ex. 1). By doing away with the filling-in arpeggios in the piano left hand

Ex. 1(a) Serenade: p. 4, bars 52–3

Ex. 1(b) *Oedipus rex*: vocal score, pp. 2–3

and replacing them with an incisive quaver oscillation (lower strings plus timpani, harp and piano), while at the same time flattening the major third into the minor, Stravinsky invented a lapidary musical equivalent for the dramatic idea of 'imploration' which dominates the opening pages of *Oedipus rex*. Several other ideas from the Serenade underwent the same kind of treatment. Oedipus's boastful 'Eg'Oedipus' at the end of his first arioso is an energetic version, complete with descending sequence, of an apparently unimportant subsidiary figure in the 'Romanza' of the piano work (Ex. 2), and there is even a striking parallel between the superficially very different openings of the two works: an abrupt gesture followed by silence followed by a double reprise of the gesture (though the Serenade, unlike the opera, continues with further reprises).

Ex. 2(a) Serenade: p. 7, bars 26–7

Ex. 2(b) Oedipus rex: vocal score, p. 10, bars 3–5

Obviously there is no similarity between the two works in respect of any dramatic content as such, or even as regards mood in general. Stravinsky simply uses ideas from the Serenade as neutral material, rather as a locksmith selects a blank for cutting into a key: not any blank will do for any key, but a blank can supply a variety of keys within one type. It was a method he applied throughout his neo-classical phase and with particular force in *Oedipus rex*, where, curiously enough, it is combined with what looks very much like its reverse (but is really a variant of the same technique): the practice of adapting blanks of his own to other people's locks.

Oedipus starts violently and without musical preliminaries, choir and orchestra attacking the downbeat together in a gesture of panic and despair. It is an opening as remote as possible from baroque oratorio, and its real inspiration seems to have come from much nearer Stravinsky's own day, from the Italian operas of which we know, from his own writings and the later testimony of Robert Craft, that he was fond. The composer himself mentions

Verdi as an influence on *Oedipus rex*, and Craft draws attention to Leonard Bernstein's observation of the connection between Stravinsky's orchestral head-motive and Aida's 'Pietà ti prenda' in the second act of Verdi's opera.[20] But while the conjunction here of an exact motivic parallel with a resemblance of dramatic situation (Aida is on her knees to Amneris) is impressive, the two phrases are hardly similar at all as musical gesture. In this respect, the first scene of *Oedipus* might more directly suggest the opening of Verdi's *Otello*. The comparison can be pursued in some detail. In both works an anxious crowd is imploring deliverance, and in both formal resolution is provided by a commanding central character (tenor solo) who presents himself as proof against the caprices of fortune but whom in reality fortune is about to bring to his knees.

Musically there are many similarities. Both works open with a tempestuous upward sweep in the orchestra followed by a pause and, later, an extended continuation controlled by ostinatos based on thirds. Stravinsky's choral head-motive (as opposed to the orchestral one preferred by Bernstein) seems to echo the rocking muted horn figure that fills the lull after Verdi's initial hurricane-force gust. But the more subliminal source of both figures is surely Gregorian chant (perhaps even the 'Dies irae'); and it is an important similarity that both openings make repeated melodic reference to plainsong, and through it to the idea of the crowd as supplicants before a priest or before God himself. Oedipus (though not Otello) tends to accept this priestly role in his arioso, which throughout suggests a highly embellished version of the kind of chant Stravinsky would once again have been encountering in the mid-twenties as a communicant of the Russian Orthodox church.

For all these various similarities, Stravinsky's opening rarely sounds specifically Verdian in the way Jocasta's aria later in the work does. This is partly because the modelling is not at the level of musical style but at the more general level of gesture and dramatic parallel. But it is also because Stravinsky typically mixes allusions in such a way as to confuse our sense of style, and because, finally, the temporal dynamic of his writing is crucially different from that of romantic Italian opera.

Compare Verdi's and Stravinsky's use of ostinato. In *Otello* the string triplets portray the ship's unseen struggle with the storm while at the same time conveying the tense anxiety of the crowd; and although Verdi's chording is in some respects radical, it maintains in general the purposeful structure of traditional tonal harmony. But Stravinsky, as usual in his neo-classical music, merely alludes to such structures without committing himself to their syntactic consequences. The ostinato passage starting at fig. 2 is, melodically, a succession of implied cadences in B♭ minor, the referential key of this whole scene. But the cadences are undermined by two essential features of Stravinsky's style: first, the oblique modality of the inner voices, which seem to vacillate arbitrarily between the sharpened and flattened leading notes (A/A♭), and to do so, moreover, in a rhythmically unpredictable way which casts doubt on the accentual coordination so vital to traditional cadencing (see Ex. 1b); secondly, the irrational numerical scheme governing the melodic phrase lengths, as against the remorselessly regular tread of the B♭/D♭ ostinato. So, while the ostinato sticks to its pattern of three-plus-three quavers, the melody (always consisting of a variable number of repeated notes ending in a three-note cadence figure) starts with the sequence 12–9–6–12–12 (quavers), which involves an intermediate change in the phasing of the two elements (compare bars 3 and 5 of Ex. 1b). This is in fact a much simplified version of procedures first worked out systematically in *The Rite of Spring*.[21] But the new tonal references ensure that its meaning is much less simple than its numerology.

The musical effect of all this is, roughly speaking, to rob the cadence of its traditional role of marking-out rhythmic and harmonic structure, and to induce a certain sense of structural inertia as a result. It is rather like a car journey in which you keep passing the same house but at slightly irregular intervals and with the chimneys in a different place each time. There is movement; and yet there is not movement. This fits very well the numbed anguish of the plague-ridden Theban people. But the technique itself is fundamental, not a mere dramatic convenience. It goes with Stravinsky's concept of theatre, and beyond that of music itself, as ritual – something, that is, which is reenacted rather than simply enacted. We shall refer again to this idea as it applies to *Oedipus rex* later in the chapter.

The ritual element in *Oedipus* brings us back meanwhile to its supposed baroque models. In gesture and dramatic language, as I suggested earlier, the opening is remote from Handelian oratorio. But there are general similarities which the eye and ear seem to record subconsciously. Whatever inspired Stravinsky's first *visual* image (of the chorus seated 'in a single row across the stage'), it does obviously suggest the curved chorus-line of an oratorio performance, with the singers reading from scrolls instead of vocal scores and wearing cowls instead of dinner jackets. In the same way the Latin text, especially if (as is likely) we cannot make it out in detail, probably reminds us of Requiem or Mass settings, if not by Handel then by Bach or perhaps even Haydn or Mozart or their contemporaries. Whether or not the first vocal figure comes from the 'Dies irae' chant, the emotional atmosphere of this whole opening is recognisably that of a choral 'Dies irae' such as Mozart's – an allusion which may also be detected in Verdi's *Otello*, though without the linguistic support.

But how far do such references penetrate into the actual structure and expressive detail of the music? The answer seems to be, not very far. The long formal structures and rigid demarcations of Handel's narrative oratorios are hinted at but scarcely observed, except partially in the arias of Creon and Jocasta. In the first scene, the true formal syntax is fluid, with Oedipus's solo contributions morticed into the choral sections by dovetailed rhythmic figures and quasi-conventional harmonic transitions. Lourié thought that the essentially static harmonies of *Oedipus rex* descended from those of Handel; and he drew attention to what he called the 'monometric' character of Stravinsky's writing, which he seems to have regarded as a kind of rhythmic correlative of the harmony.[22] But Stravinsky's harmonies are static because functionless, whereas Handel's are static (if at all) because they function within a restricted set of terms, as does a great deal of baroque music. As for the monometrics, this had been a preoccupation of Stravinsky's since *The Rite of Spring*, and is best understood as a way of establishing complex metric relationships through unified rhythmic values, whereas in baroque and indeed classical music the relationship between the unified value and the metre is axiomatic (for instance, it explains the word 'movement' as describing a single, self-contained musical piece within a larger work). In the first scene of *Oedipus* completely different metres are linked by common values (as shown in Ex. 3), in a way radically at odds with baroque practice. It may be true that Stravinsky had, in the early twenties, sensed some parallel between this idea and the supposed 'knitting-needle' aspects of baroque rhythm (just as it had a little earlier prompted an interest in ragtime). But its real origins, for him, lay in the ostinato rhythmic patterns of his early ballets, and, through them, in the desire to substitute precisely notated mechanisms for the swooning rubatos of the late romantics.

Even so, the idea of baroque formality seems to have been in his mind, as a point of reference, while he was composing *Oedipus*. It surfaces here and there in an isolated figure, like the unexpected descending sequence in the chorus basses at fig. 10, or the dotted semiquaver motif that links the 'E peste' chorus to Oedipus's 'Liberi' aria, or the somewhat patterned use of melodic suspension in the aria itself. But these devices are invariably more or less deceptive. The 'E peste' chorus itself is a kind of mock fugato, turning the obsessive repetitions of the preceding chorus into a litany. But while the writing here (including the instrumental parts) is genuinely contrapuntal in

Ex. 3 p. 12

NB All page references are to the vocal score unless indicated otherwise

that the parts move independently of one another, apparently creating the harmony as they go, Stravinsky studiously sabotages the fugal imitation itself by transferring the melodic imitation to the leading voice (the basses) at the crucial moment (Ex. 4). Why does he do this? Obviously, to avoid the problem of vocal tessitura created by his choice of the octave as imitative interval. But then why choose the octave? The answer may lie in the semiquaver horn chords (fig. 11), which persist in an ostinato chordal pattern based on the alternation of the notes D♯ and C♯. If this ostinato is the underlying idea of the passage, then it supports Lourié in his observation that 'here polyphony is limited to the adumbration of predetermined harmonies which are dictated and imposed on it in advance'.[23] The counterpoint does not govern the harmony after all, but is governed by it, despite the brilliantly engineered effect to the contrary.

Ex. 4 p. 6 (accompaniment omitted)

Vale, Creo!

After Oedipus's second aria ('Uxoris frater'), Creon himself appears and announces, as the Speaker informs us, that the Oracle demands the tracking down and expulsion of Laius's murderer, who is hiding in Thebes. The chorus's shouts of 'Vale, Creo!'[24] introduce G major in the guise of the dominant of C major, the key of Creon's aria; and it is important that the narration (unaccompanied) comes between this chord and its resolution, so that what the Speaker has to say is carried on musically into the aria, while leaping ahead of it by anticipating Oedipus's reply. Notice that this is not an isolated effect, but is set up by the 'Uxoris frater' monologue, which makes a much-embroidered but perfectly clear stepwise melodic descent from the tenor's and violins' Gb (itself prepared by a solo cello) to the middle C on which Creon is about to enter. At the same time the orchestral bass (solo cello, then horn) also descends by step from Ab towards the subdominant F preceding the dominant chord itself.

As described in words, this would sound to a music-theorist like a textbook sequence of fourth species suspensions leading to a IV–V–I cadence in C. But the reality (Ex. 5) is very different. The two parts proceed like blind men groping their way down a narrow staircase, keeping as close together as they dare and sometimes bumping into each other or tripping over each other's legs. The image of Oedipus's moral blindness could hardly be more poignant,

Ex. 5 pp. 12–13, 15 (abstract)

in this context where systematic voice-leading seems to be the intention; nor could the contrast with Creon, a military man of positively Offenbachian fatuity, whose C major is the mental world of a soldier prepared to blunder through any (tonal) difficulty so long as he comes out still in C major. Stravinsky himself referred to the 'Folies Bergères' tune at fig. 40, perhaps deliberately overlooking its descent from Glazunov (a detested older pupil of Rimsky-Korsakov), as well as the whole French satirical tradition from Chabrier to Poulenc. But in any case the obvious intention is to make an ass – perhaps a dangerous ass – of Creon, contrasting him once again with the more subtle, though deluded, Oedipus, whose 'Non reperias' (in C minor/ E♭ major) starts hesitantly and only regains his earlier self-assurance at 'Miki debet se dedere',[25] where he at first, somewhat vaguely, echoes the chorus's words 'tibi dixit' (the God spoke to *you*) before firmly correcting himself: 'you must have faith in *me*'.

Though cast in the form of an aria (with choral interjections), 'Non reperias'

Ex. 6 p. 25

lacks the motivic coherence we associate with that genre in classical or Italian romantic opera. It seems literally to be engaged in a search, and the musical images vary with Oedipus's feelings about that quest, and with the somewhat erratic pattern of poetic line repetition in which he expresses them. In general, throughout *Oedipus rex*, musical figures attach themselves to particular words or phrases. Here, for instance, the recurrent word 'Thebes' nearly always asserts the note E♭, often reinforced by its dominant (B♭); 'eruam' ('I will search out') is invariably set to the same peremptory triplet figure, at once repeated; 'Miki debet se dedere' has its own figure, which does not survive the verbal phrase, though interestingly the falling semiquavers of 'debet' invert into rising semiquavers for 'debet se dedere' and the figure then attaches itself to 'deferre', a procedure which suggests that it is sometimes the sounds of the words, as much as their meaning or context, that suggest the musical motifs. But the final section, where Oedipus boasts of his riddle-solving powers, establishes a more settled scheme and tonality, with the self-regarding arabesques of the 'Liberi' monologue returning to embellish each phrase. Even here, though, the musical recurrence is controlled by a verbal motif: the words 'solvi' ('I solved'), 'divinabo' ('I shall deduce') and the rhyming 'servabo' ('I shall save' [Thebes]) prompt the same falling semitone combined with a durational accent (Ex. 6). It is not necessary to understand such patterns in terms of a specific symbolic 'meaning' in order to accept that the verbal and poetic schemes are at the bottom of the musical ones.

This second scene ends, like the first, with choral acclamations, this time in the form of a short antiphon, in which the 'priest' Oedipus answers the shouts of 'solve!' with his ceremonial promise in plainsong over a deep pedal

Eb, which is then held under the ensuing narration. Thus there is a kind of structural 'rhyme' between the two scenes, clinched by the fact that the third scene begins with the minor-third ostinato music from the start of the work (but now a semitone higher in B minor). Meanwhile, the Speaker, in describing how Tiresias is stung into his accusation of Oedipus by Oedipus's own accusation against him, for the first time declaims rhythmically, setting the ominous words 'roi est un roi' to the rhythm of the ostinato. Since this is the chorus's motif of 'imploration' (originally of Oedipus, now of Tiresias), the omniscient Speaker is indicating that the question contains its own answer, a point emphasised by the fact that the two different kings he mentions have occupied the same throne (as well as the same wife). So Oedipus's very first claim, 'I shall free you from the plague', will prove more literally true than he yet knows.

The oracle speaks

From the narrative point of view, the third and final scene of Act I is one of the most confused in the work. As we saw in chapter 2, the Speaker gives a muddled account of its sequence of events, stating wrongly that Tiresias's outburst follows Oedipus's allegation that he and Creon are conspiring to seize his throne. What really happens (in the Latin text and Sophocles) is that Oedipus accuses Tiresias of the *murder*, whereupon Tiresias counter-accuses Oedipus, and Oedipus only then alleges a plot against his throne. In Sophocles, he repeats this accusation to Creon (whom he also accuses of Laius's murder), and there then follows the quarrel to which the Speaker and Jocasta both refer in the next scene, but which otherwise does not figure in Stravinsky's work.

No doubt Stravinsky left out the quarrel because he wanted to avoid at this point the conventional operatic action-dialogue, complete with its associated repertoire of gestures. This is certainly borne out by the way he in fact set the scene. It consists of four quite distinct elements: the chorus urging Tiresias to speak; Tiresias's aria, interrupted only momentarily by Oedipus's accusation of murder; Oedipus's own aria 'Invidia fortunam odit', in which he accuses Creon and Tiresias of plotting against his throne; and the final chorus of welcome to Jocasta. There is no better expression of Stravinsky's powerfully disengaged style of musical dramaturgy than this utterly formal handling of a scene which, even in Sophocles, is so essentially dynamic and dialectical.

The formality is enhanced by the fact that both choruses belong, in a sense, elsewhere. The first, as we have just seen, brings back the opening chorus of

Ex. 7 pp. 39–40

the work, albeit with much striking variation of detail (notice, for instance, how the change from a minor third to a perfect fourth in the ostinato figure at fig. 65 seems to mark an increased urgency in the people's demands for a resolution). The last chorus refers not backwards but forwards, to the next scene, where we shall in fact hear it again. But its contrast with the end of Oedipus's aria is nevertheless shrewdly calculated. In his final C minor phrase the king broods obsessively on the imagined plot against him, rocking back and forth between E♭ and C; the chorus then burst in thrillingly in C major, welcoming the real threat to Oedipus, in the person of his wife/mother (Ex. 7). It is worth comparing the effect of this juxtaposition with two outstanding precedents: the end of Act I of Wagner's *Tristan* (also C major), and the end of the ball scene in Tchaikovsky's *Queen of Spades* (D major). Stravinsky seems able to achieve a more disturbing irony by virtue of the disjunct character of his design. The Romantics' need to compose the contrast into the texture, so to speak, weakens the effect by drawing attention to the contrivance involved.

The bass Tiresias's aria, like Creon's, is his sole contribution to the work. It is notable for its lack of superficial variety or even interest; and for the significant fact that its dramatic high point – the unmasking of Laius's murderer – is allowed at first to pass with no more than discreet compositional emphasis in the middle of the aria (the actual word 'peremptor' – 'murderer' – is marked with dynamic accents, and the bass ostinato goes down an octave). Tiresias is an old man, blind and therefore, paradoxically, a seer.[26] Like Pimen in Mussorgsky's *Boris Godunov*, he speaks slowly, evenly (in regular note values and phrase lengths) and without passion, even when provoked by Oedipus's absurd and ill-considered accusation. He is accompanied with extreme simplicity (at first by plain bassoon scales with a stately octave figure on violins) until his response to Oedipus, 'Miserande, dico', where a wind chord of unforgettable radiance announces the impending prophecy, a device which recalls Mozart's use of wind instruments at moments of solemnity. By contrast, Oedipus's 'Invidia fortunam odit' ('Envy hates good fortune') is, like his 'Non reperias', musically and psychologically unsettled. At the start the voice slips in quietly on Tiresias's final D, at once treating it as a leading-note appoggiatura in the key of E♭, so that the vocal line takes on a yearning, striving quality somewhat at odds with the blunt manner of the text.[27]

As a musical design, too, 'Invidia fortunam odit' resembles 'Non reperias' in the strict relationship between its verbal and musical phrases. Each musical image attaches to a single line of text, and is always and only (with a single exception) repeated with that text. But this in fact applies to only two phrases: the opening 'Invidia fortunam odit' itself, and the next line, 'Creavistis me regem' ('you made me king').[28] Other phrases occur only singly, and here Stravinsky does not necessarily regard individual word-repeats as motivic: so, for instance, the words 'solvendum' and 'solvatum' do not call up musical similarities, as they might do in Wagner, even though they allude always to the same fact: that it was Oedipus, not Tiresias, who solved the riddle of the Sphinx. This contrasts with 'Non reperias', where, as we saw, Stravinsky does sometimes equate words of similar sound, even when there is no association of meaning.

One wonders whether this apparently somewhat mechanical repetition procedure was suggested by the baroque aria formula in which three or four lines of text are made to serve, more or less arbitrarily, for several pages of music. Certainly the way in which familiar phrases crop up, apparently at random, in mid-aria does recall this old Metastasian habit. But Stravinsky's procedure is less unsystematic than it looks. The text of 'Invidia fortunam odit' is like a gradual act of memory in which Oedipus casts his mind farther and farther back to the events which led to his becoming King of Thebes, while the repeated lines assert, in their logical place, the present consequences of those events. Memory – his own, the Messenger's, the Shepherd's – is to be the key to Oedipus's fate, the process which will explain and resolve the confusions of the present time. So in building on a loose stream of associations coming back again and again to what Oedipus believes to be the certainties of here and now – 'envy hates the fortunate', 'you made me king' – the aria achieves not only a brilliant, quasi-formal musical design, but also a dramatically telling picture of self-assurance gradually undermined by the Truth, which is the apparent significance of Oedipus's pathetic C minor phrase 'Volunt regem perire' so grossly juxtaposed with the C major chorus of welcome to Jocasta (see Ex. 7).

The parting of the ways

Oedipus rex is nominally a two-act opera, and at the end of the chorus the curtain is supposed to fall. When it rises on Act II, we are supposed to hear the same chorus once again, followed by the Speaker's introduction and Jocasta's aria 'Nonn'erubeskite'. But in fact hardly anyone ever performs *Oedipus* with an interval, nor does it look as if that was Stravinsky's intention. The device of the false interval comes from Cocteau's *Orphée*, where, between the identical Scenes viii and viii*bis*, 'the interval curtain falls slowly then at once rises again'. The repeated scene stands for the passage of time during which Orphée descends to Hades and intercedes with Death for the return of Eurydice, a time described to him by Heurtebise as 'Long . . . for you. For us, you will do hardly more than enter and leave'. It fits, that is, into the interstices between an event and the selfsame event. In *Oedipus*, admittedly, there is no obvious equivalent signification, and the repeat looks more like a device to suggest unbroken continuity after a scene change, since the preface to the score demands a new backcloth and the removal of the decorative draperies from Act I. Unfortunately, Stravinsky's own exact intentions are unclear. In the score, the sequence is as given above, and suggests a simple overlap between the end of Act I and the start of Act II. But in *Dialogues* (p. 29), he advocates delaying the repeat of the chorus until after the Speaker's introduction, 'because I prefer to go directly, without narration, from tutti G major to *solo* flute and harp G minor'. And this is indeed what he did in his 1962 Washington recording, made at about the time of the *Dialogues* conversation. The new sequence produces a magnificent irony as the Speaker's 'he is afraid' is directly followed by the brilliant chorus.[29] But it weakens the continuity effect, which is made imprecise by the intrusion of the Speaker. The truth is probably that the device was used by Cocteau for reasons of stylisation, and was then modified in performance by Stravinsky on practical grounds. The score offers an 'ideal' version which, in practice, is rarely followed.

The stage is now set for the longest vocal solo, indeed the longest musical 'number' in the work. Queen Jocasta, like Creon and Tiresias, sings only in the one scene, and like them she has a significance that is partly emblematic. She is, so to speak, at once the grandeur and the falsehood of Oedipus's position. Untroubled by his dawning sense of guilt or his growing desire for clarity, she is at first haughtily dismissive of oracles then later anxious to evade the whole issue. She is, we feel, one of those aristocrats who believe in structures rather than truths, and this makes her incautious. Her proof of the mendaciousness of oracles is lethal to Oedipus's case. Laius, she says, was supposed to be killed by her son, but in fact he was killed by robbers at a crossing of three roads ('trivium'). Oedipus at once remembers his own encounter with an old man at a road junction, and insists on speaking with the sole survivor of the old man's retinue, while Jocasta wants only to draw him away, to discourage his sudden zest for truth.

This first and only appearance of any female voice in *Oedipus rex* has an immediately electrifying effect on its atmosphere. By placing her intervention at the start of the second act, Stravinsky makes it feel like the turning-point of the whole drama. Jocasta will calm the situation and bring to it a fresh sense of proportion; her opening harp chord is at once an index of her standing and dignity, but it also has a suggestion of bardic insight, a sense of tapping down to deep and ancient roots. Of all the arias in *Oedipus rex*, it is perhaps this one which most brilliantly conveys the richness and complexity of the drama of great souls brought low by human frailty. With all her grandeur and emotional maturity, Jocasta is in fact powerless to alter the course of events which she either cannot or will not comprehend. Her words show her inability to face reality, for we know that in repudiating oracles she is being less than candid, having herself set in train this entire sequence of events precisely out of fear of one. Here, more than anywhere, Daniélou's brilliant Latin text conveys the terrible emptiness and helplessness of human social forms in the face of divine retribution. Jocasta, masked, immobile, and trapped in a dead language, might be the original of Lear's 'as flies to wanton boys, are we to the gods; they kill us for their sport'.

If that were the whole story, we might well regard her as little more than an object of passing curiosity, an exotic but tattered butterfly pinned to a card and exhibited in some dusty glass-fronted cabinet. But *Oedipus rex* is a music drama, and it is in her music that Jocasta takes shape as a properly rounded *dramatis persona*. The extra dimension is apparent in her very first phrase, with its accompaniment for three flutes added to the harp. Though they play few notes, the flutes hint at a discreet sensuality as they brush lightly against a mezzo-soprano line that is itself as sinuous and suggestive as the verbal language is flat and dispassionate. Later, Jocasta launches into a neo-Verdian aria which seems to imply that her sensuality is worn out, like her cheeks which she tries despairingly to rejuvenate in the penultimate act of Cocteau's later Oedipus play *La Machine infernale*. Later still, in the vivo section of the aria and in her Tempo agitato duet with Oedipus, fear and even panic break through the cold lapidary surface of the stage idiom and the superficial stylisation of the music. By the end of the scene Jocasta's musical persona has digressed so far from the statuesque idea that supposedly controls the work as to generate a sense of suppressed violence by no means wholly unlike the brutality that is never far beneath the controlled surface of Sophocles himself.

What are the musical elements in this remarkable *tour de force*? The Verdian model of the main slow 'Nonn'erubeskite' section is patent enough. What may be less obvious, because partly disguised by the over-all stylistic context, is the fact that the introduction, up to fig. 96, refers once again to baroque music: not Handel this time, however, but the Bach of the contemplative *ariosi* in the passion settings. As always with Stravinsky, the allusion is oblique. It works through the idea of accompanied recitative, with the voice entering at once after an initial pedal chord; through the smooth, unhurried quaver pulse, and especially through the somewhat vagrant harmony, a feature of Bach's ariosos which gives them their particular quality of frail human quest. After the imperfect cadence in E♭ minor just before 96, the music sideslips back to the initial G minor, and at the same time makes an abrupt somersault into the stylistic world of the 'Lacrymosa' in Verdi's *Requiem*, complete with four-bar phrases and slow oom-chah accompaniment (Ex. 8). But unlike any normal Verdi aria (and once again closer to baroque models), Jocasta's is in ternary form, with a quick bipartite middle section containing her warning about oracles, followed by a da capo reprise of the main slow music, which dovetails into Oedipus's 'Pavesco subito' and the agitated duet that concludes the scene. It is this duet that fulfils the more conventional Verdian function of the cabaletta, which modified the old bravura conclusion into a device for reestablishing dramatic urgency after a reflective or introspective aria. A glance through any middle-period Verdi opera will show how closely Stravinsky's scheme reflects the mature Verdian way of breathing dramatic life into a rigid and artificial formal convention. Intending to reassure him, Jocasta destroys her husband with a single word ('trivium' – the fork in the

Ex. 8 p. 44

Nonn' e - ru - be - ski - te in ae -gra u - rbe cla - ma - re,

road where Oedipus killed Laius); and from anger, Oedipus plunges to fear and anxious questioning, a mood exactly caught by the disturbed quaver triplets of the duet. But this rapid psychological evolution is contained by a formal scheme which intensifies the feeling that the characters are in the grip of inexorable forces.

One must add that this idea is hardly Stravinsky's invention. Verdi used it with equal power in, for example, 'Ah fors' é lui' at the end of Act I of *La Traviata*, where the regular two-verse aria-cabaletta form ending with a duet subtly insists that Violetta's freedom – though asserted with such musical bravura – is illusory.

Is Jocasta then a neo-Verdian heroine? It would surely be more helpful to suggest that Verdi was for Stravinsky the model for a more generalised quality of 'operatic-ness' which he wanted as a supporting context for his classical drama. In a short article published a few months after the first performance of *Oedipus rex*, Stravinsky referred to 'a deeper search than the simple imitation of language'.[30] In his instrumental works of the early twenties, that search seems to have been for musical meanings and allusions to replace the lost continuity of history and, in Stravinsky's case, geography as well. That the models were studiously well-ordered ones was part of the common movement towards 'reconstruction'. But a Sophoclean drama made more complex demands, not least because the urge to write once more for the theatre was itself apparently some kind of reaction to the hard matter-of-factness of the instrumental scores.

It looks, then, as if Stravinsky wanted an enrichment of the coolly objective patterns suggested by his original ideas for a Latin text and a constructivist *mise en scène*, and found it in the passionate, larger-than-life, but essentially conventional idiom of the nineteenth-century Italian musical stage. It was crucial to this choice that Stravinsky himself loved Verdi and attended his operas on every possible occasion;[31] that behind all the ham emotionalism and spurious realism of works like *Il Trovatore* and *Aida*, Verdi was a highly formal artist with a respect for convention and a genius for artifice somewhat akin to Stravinsky's own.[32] But at the same time the 'ham' elements have also to be reckoned with. Stravinsky certainly was not unaware of Verdi's reputation for coarseness. On the contrary, it was precisely the crudities of Verdian style that he was at pains to imitate: the square phrases, oom-chah accompaniments and absurdly plain harmonies, the clarinets in thirds and sixths, the chromatic scales and shock-horror diminished seventh chords.[33] These are the unmistakable signals of routine Italianism, where more subtle quotation might well pass unnoticed. Clearly Stravinsky wanted us to understand his characters partly as refugees from the Verdian stage, whose masks conceal, not the cold immobile beauty of Greek statues, but grimaces which we, when we go to the opera, accept as the outward sign of an emotion too great to be borne in silence. In other words, it is the simple directness and sheer force of operatic feeling which Stravinsky wanted to suggest as attributes of these statuesque victims of the most horrendous moral torments yet devised by speculative man. And if this entailed intimations of vulgarity, so much the better. What fiercer challenge could there be to the self-congratulatory primness of a classical education than the thought that Oedipus's conceit and fear, Jocasta's evasiveness, Tiresias's anger, might be on much the same emotional level as Violetta's self-sacrifice or Amneris's vindictiveness, to say nothing of Verdi's own grief at the death of Manzoni?

One needs, admittedly, to insist on that 'might be'. Whatever else *Oedipus rex* may be, it is not imitation Verdi. Not only are the references oblique and often fragmentary, but they are also, as we have seen, mixed with others of a quite different character and all are strongly mediated by Stravinskyisms. This whole scene, indeed, could be taken as a model of the synthetic approach in *Oedipus rex* generally. Take the Verdi-isms in 'Nonn'erubeskite' (see Ex. 8). They boil down to a textural/rhythmic figure carrying the harmony, combined with a certain style of ornamented vocal melody, four-square phrasing, and some incidental details of scoring. But the harmonic figure at once produces a Stravinskyism, in the shape of a bass-line which candidly disregards the precepts of the simple, highly conventionalised Italian style. Ex. 9 suggests how a 'correct' bass-line might proceed (though this is already adventurous by Italian standards).

The striking thing is that, in pure harmonic terms, Stravinsky's bass is only

Ex. 9 p. 44 (accompaniment modified)

very subtly 'wrong', though it is also, as a musical line, unidiomatic, since it mainly obeys 'top-line' rules of motion by step, and ignores the strong tonic-dominant motion that would invariably be reflected in an Italian operatic bass-line. This procedure is quite in keeping with Stravinsky's normal melodic technique, derived originally, it seems, from modal folk-tunes. Such melodies keep in close position, and return persistently to one or two focal notes which are felt to be embellished by the notes around them. Jocasta's own vocal line here is in that vein, despite its obvious feints towards cadential tonality. Though harmonisable, it has a shape akin to that of a folk-song embellishing the note G, which is why it fails to insist on an obvious bass-line as a Verdi melody would do. Verdi also sometimes wrote highly focused and motivic tunes of this kind (a well-known example is 'Addio del passato', in Act III of *La Traviata*); but their patterning is invariably dictated by the conventions of tonal harmony. In 'Addio del passato' the harmony is entirely V–I (in the tonic or the relative major), except in the visionary tonic major section, which introduces modestly vagrant elements. In general this is as much a case of melodisable harmony as of harmonisable melody.

The point having been made, the rest of Jocasta's aria largely abandons the Verdian model (except, of course, for the da capo, which is a literal repeat). The Vivo middle section at fig. 100, with its bravura clarinet arpeggios, follows late eighteenth-century formulae (those of Mozart's *Requiem* rather than Verdi's), while the frenzied duet grafts on to this stock a kind of wild Rossinian patter which introduces an element of the grotesque into Jocasta's self-delusion, highlit by prominent scoring for that ostentatiously unclassical instrument, the E♭ clarinet. In these quick sections Jocasta takes on certain musical attributes of the Queen of the Night. Her repeated-note 'oracula' recalls the sinister head-motive of 'Der Hölle Rache', and also 'Nur stille, stille', in Act II of *The Magic Flute*. But the figure is conventional, and might have any number of classical forebears. Stravinsky, unclassically, infests the whole orchestra with it, and later it echoes menacingly in the figure for the word 'trivium', an obsessive treatment which seems to locate the chorus, who sing it, firmly within Oedipus's own guilty brain. Musically these patterns, like the so-called motor rhythms of the contemporary instrumental works, are simply a classicised version of the irregular ostinato figures so characteristic of the early ballets. But the composer would surely have been less pleased at the suggestion that the *dramatic* technique here is essentially Wagnerian. The rhythmic leitmotif links the trigger-word 'trivium' to the oracle whose prophecy it fulfils, and later, in Oedipus's ceremonial confession (at fig. 119), to the crucial act of murder ('kekidi'). This important idea, with its associated methodology, continues into the next scene; and it is in fact one of the chief devices by which Stravinsky sustains the dramatic tension from Oedipus's first tremor of foreboding ('Pavesco subito'), to the culminating moment of truth at 'Lux facta est' (Ex. 10).

Lux facta est

Some such device seems to have been needed particularly because musically the ensuing scene of the Messenger and the Shepherd demanded a change of tone, one which, on the face of it, might have implied a relaxation in the tension just when, dramatically, it had to be increased. The witness who 'steps from the shadows' at this point is, as we saw earlier, not the Messenger but the Shepherd who in Sophocles escaped from the scene of Laius's murder. Returning to Thebes and finding Oedipus already king, the man lied to Creon

Ex. 10

about the number of Laius's assailants and begged Jocasta to send him as her shepherd far from the city. But the Messenger had also been a shepherd, tending flocks on the mountain where the baby Oedipus was to have been abandoned by his parents. In the play he identifies the other shepherd (the survivor from the murder) as the very man who had originally handed the baby to him, having balked at killing the child as ordered. The Messenger/ Shepherd had then taken Oedipus to Corinth, where Polybus had adopted him.[34]

The pastoral motif is central to this whole scene, and gives it both musically and dramatically a unique character. Messengers and shepherds are archetypal. The messenger, by definition, has special knowledge which may possibly alter the course of events. The shepherd – 'omniskius pastor', as the chorus call him at the start of the scene – stands apart from ordinary social intercourse and is uninfluenced by the follies of urban man. He too is felt to know and understand better than the rest of us, because his life is led close to nature and in conditions of hardship and self-abnegation. But the shepherd has also another significance, due to his particular trade. Like the shepherds at the Nativity, or the shepherd in *The Winter's Tale*, or the shepherd Dionysus in Szymanowski's *King Roger*, Jocasta's shepherd is a symbol of rebirth, a kind of spiritual midwife. 'Thou mettest with things dying,' says Shakespeare's old shepherd to his son, 'I with things new-born.' And the rescue of the baby Perdita is indeed the moral turning point of that wonderful play. So too in *Oedipus rex*, the appearance of the shepherd marks the point at which Oedipus can no longer doubt that he has, however unwittingly, committed a heinous crime against nature, for which he must atone. The Messenger is unaware of this, and knows no more than that Oedipus need not fear Corinth, since Polybus was only his adoptive father ('falsus pater'). But the Shepherd knows all, and asks only that he be permitted to remain silent. Or, to be exact, Cocteau has him speak the truth while several times asserting that the truth should not be spoken, an inevitably somewhat confusing condensation of the scene in Sophocles where Oedipus drags the truth out of him by threats of torture and death.

Stravinsky's music is dominated by the Messenger's bucolic solo, 'Reppereram in monte puerum Oedipoda' and the Shepherd's brief 'A patre, a matre, in monte derelictum', accompanied only by two bassoons in the character of an alpine *ranz des vaches*. But everything in the scene reflects the new pastoral atmosphere: the feeling of great space and spiritual isolation. The orchestra is almost throughout reduced to a minimum. The opening chorus, announcing the arrival of the Shepherd and the Messenger, is for a time unaccompanied, even though the male voices are often in unison or two parts; the Messenger's solo, with its discreetly barbaric rhythms (because the Messenger is a foreigner?), is lightly touched in by strings, and later, in the section where the chorus interpret Oedipus's having been found on a mountainside as a sign of divine parentage, the theme itself is picked up quietly by a sextet of wind instruments who invest it with a mysterious radiance, as if confirming the gods' interest in Oedipus's case. Finally, Oedipus's own reply, the aria 'Nonne monstrum reskituri', is supported in little more than fragmentary fashion, as if even the instruments of the orchestra had deserted him: cor anglais and bassoon, then cellos, a solo trumpet and timpani softly doubling a cello/bass ostinato. Not until the Shepherd and the Messenger together pronounce the charge against Oedipus – 'son of Laius and Jocasta, murderer of his parent Laius, husband of his parent Jocasta' – is there anything like an orchestral fortissimo, and it is shortlived. Oedipus's own 'Lux facta est' – 'light has dawned' – is uttered in near silence before, for the first time in the work, he leaves the stage.[35]

It seems typical of Stravinsky that both texture and form should be at their most economical for this moment of dramatic truth. The concise introduction, with its curious sense of puzzlement arising perhaps from something scattered and indecisive about the accompaniment, leads in two verses ('Polybus is dead' and 'He was not Oedipus's true father') to a series of strict ternary-form solos: the Messenger's, the Shepherd's and Oedipus's, each advancing the drama swiftly but with a certain lugubrious formality, like the proceedings in a court room. The knot is then tied by a varied duo reprise (Messenger, Shepherd) of the Messenger's solo, again in A–B–A form but with the B section this time consisting of the actual charge against Oedipus, so that the curious situation arises of a melodramatic climax followed by a reprise of earlier material obviously calculated to restrain and formalise its effect – the most striking example of a device adopted on more than one occasion in *Oedipus rex*. Finally, in the sublime coda, Oedipus's threefold 'confession' – 'I was born against divine law; I married against divine law; I killed against divine law' – balances the threefold charge against him.

All this is bound together by a tight tonal structure, in which the Messenger's G minor (the same key as Jocasta's, as confirmed by the pedal G that underpins the Speaker's link between the two scenes) proceeds to a complex but unmistakable dominant (D minor/major–B minor) for the charge, the confession and the 'Lux facta est'. But if there is tonal symbolism here, as convincingly argued many years ago by Wilfrid Mellers,[36] it is surely overshadowed by the more concrete symbolism of the musical materials and the varied harmonic colouring. The pastoral modality is not shared by the chorus, except when they take up the Messenger's music at fig. 144, nor by Oedipus himself in his somewhat foolish and light-headed F major aria, whose first phrase reminded Eric Walter White of one of the Lanner waltzes in *Petrushka* but Stravinsky himself apparently of Beckmesser's lute song in Act II of *Die Meistersinger*, especially perhaps the second line with its characteristic and studiously 'weak' emphasis on the sixth and fourth of the scale (Ex. 11).[37] Does Oedipus also resemble Beckmesser in his impenetrable conceit? The idea is distasteful, because Oedipus lacks Beckmesser's conscious will to deceive and does gradually seek out and yield to the evidence of his own inadequacy. But 'Nonne monstrum' is undoubtedly his frailest moment. Faced by the news of his adoptive upbringing, which in Greek eyes would make him an upstart, he seems ready to accept the chorus's view that his birth was miraculous. But the real dramatic cue is Jocasta's sudden, silent exit at the end of the Shepherd's solo. She now knows the truth, from the Shepherd's description of the child Oedipus abandoned with his feet pierced by thongs. Oedipus

Ex. 11(a) Wagner, *Die Meistersinger von Nürnberg*, Act II

"Den Tag seh' ich er - schein - en,

blau,

Ex. 11(b) *Oedipus rex*: p. 73

Non - ne mon - strum re - ski - tu - ri,

prefers to explain her departure as a snobbish reaction to his presumably humble birth. But the music lacks conviction and authority, and parades few of those melismatic flourishes which earlier seemed to burst out from Oedipus's pride and self-importance. The one on 'skiam' ('I will know') is an exception which draws attention to itself, since he does surely already know and needs time only to organise his knowledge. But the final roulade on 'Ego exul exsulto' – 'I, an exile, exult' – is a wicked verbal and musical tease at the expense of man's ability to find virtue in his own defects, for it is precisely because Oedipus is not after all an exile now that his fate as a future exile is sealed.

In one other detail the music mocks the king's attempts at self-reassurance. The dotted figure on the first clarinet, also on the word 'skiam', sounds familiar and is: it originally introduced and accompanied Oedipus's first and proudest aria, 'Liberi, vos liberabo'. Here, perhaps, it confirms that he is indeed about to release the Thebans from their torment, if not precisely in the way he can have expected.

But why does this music give an impression of smugness, and what is its significance? Harmonically, the scene is set by the chorus, 'Adest omniskius pastor', with its accumulations of chordal and melodic thirds. In tonal theory, the interval of the third is fundamental, since chords in general are thought of as based on compilations of that interval in its various forms. But the structure of tonal chords is indissolubly bound up with their grammatical function within the system, whereas – as we saw earlier – Stravinsky is much less interested in tonal functions than in tonal imagery.[38] So the strings of thirds in 'Adest omniskius pastor' and the next chorus, 'Verus non fuerat', have the patterned and elemental smoothness, but not the logical design, one associates with such schemes in classical tonality. It is true that a certain air of expectancy is generated by adding the thirds up to make sevenths (for instance at 'pater Oedipodis' and 'Falsus pater'), a type of chord that normally goes with a strong sense of impending closure at tonal cadences. But a still stronger impression in the present case is of a mechanical and essentially aimless formality, as in the 'Alberti-bass' horn figure and offbeat C major trombone scale that accompany the Messenger's (also scalar) announcement that Polybus was Oedipus's adoptive father (Ex. 12). The Messenger appears at first as a functionary carrying out a routine ceremony, quite unaware that his message will cause dismay (in Sophocles he goes so far as to announce Polybus's death as good news, since it makes Oedipus king of Corinth; and Jocasta, of course, *takes* it as good news, because she assumes it means that Oedipus's father has died a natural death).

In 'Nonne monstrum reskituri', the thirds are more systematically bound together by means of another routine technique of tonal music, the sequence, and there is perhaps greater finality in the treatment of key (for instance in the two bars before fig. 154). But even here the impression of tonal structuring is quite delusory. On the contrary, every detail contributes to the tragic picture of a man reduced to hiding his spiritual bankruptcy behind a crumbling facade

Ex. 12 p. 67

of linguistic conveniences. Take the first section down to fig. 154. It consists of two four-bar phrases in almost exact tonal sequence, followed in classic fashion by an eight-bar answering phrase ending in a tonic cadence. But the cadence is studiously deprived of meaning, by leaving the actual note of resolution (the F) off the end of the vocal figure, and by curtailing the final 2/4 bar, so that the neat tonal phrase-structure is pushed over as easily as a toy policeman with a broken foot (Ex. 13a). The music continues (at 154) with further routine patterns of sequential thirds (in which Oedipus comments, rather casually it may seem, on Jocasta's abrupt departure), and then with a slightly freer passage which, however, mercilessly satirises Oedipus's forensic ambitions by three cunningly linked musical devices: the utterly commonplace setting of the word 'skiam' ('I shall know'), the ironic appearance of the clarinet's dotted ('Liberabo') figure, and the twisting of the conventional cello and bass quaver accompaniment into a mechanical series of three-beat ostinatos, alternately on A–C and G–B – a pattern which doubly undermines the music's simple implications by refusing to descend to the strongly implied F–A, and by cutting across its two-beat metre (Ex. 13b). Simple language reduced to a meaningless routine is a potent image of human folly, suitably enshrined in da capo form, that ultimate symbol of the power of convention over individuality.

When the Messenger and the Shepherd sing, however, a different kind of simplicity comes to the fore. The patterning of the Messenger's 'Reppereram in monte puerum' is that of earlier works with connotations of primitive ritual: *The Rite of Spring*, *Les Noces*, perhaps the *Symphonies of wind instruments*. The pitch structures are modal (extended Dorian), the melodic shapes and

Ex. 13(a) p. 73

Ex. 13(b) p. 74

embellishments are those of folksong, and the metre, with its floating accent allied to an incisive pulse, harks back directly to Stravinsky's early ideas of ritual dance. The Messenger speaks, so to say, earth language, and he does it not in da capo but refrain form, which is the form of ritual and incantatory speech. Significantly, Stravinsky had several thoughts about how to bar this music, as Ex. 14 shows. Note the shift to a downbeat accent in the revised form of fig. 144, and the much broader barring scheme for this music in both versions, as compared with the original form of the idea at fig. 139. Such differences recall the barring changes in the various editions of *The Rite of Spring*, one of which was actually in hand when Stravinsky started work on *Oedipus rex*.

Ex. 14(a) (1948): p. 68

Ex. 14(b) (1928): p. 67

Ex. 14(c) (1948): p. 69

The Shepherd, on the other hand, perhaps surprisingly adopts the more conventional simplicity of western rustic art. His song is a siciliana in B♭ minor, in the traditional pastoral manner of eighteenth-century opera and oratorio, though the connection is somewhat disguised by the static *ranz des vaches* of the accompanying pair of bassoons, which replaces any kind of harmonisation as such. This accompaniment consists of a one-bar figure repeated absolutely mechanically throughout the main siciliana section of the piece. If one should wonder why the mechanical does not carry here the signification of meaningless routine it implies in Oedipus's 'Nonne monstrum', the answer might be that in the Shepherd's song the mechanical is apt to the context. It suggests the idea of a bagpipe drone, such as is often found in eighteenth-century sicilianas (like the 'pifa' in Handel's *Messiah*). But it also reminds us of the serene nature of the shepherd's calling, his remoteness from the rough and tumble of daily life, and the cold desolation of his own familiar world – the world to which, moreover, the infant Oedipus was abandoned by his fearful parents, a world beyond human choice or influence. The simplicity of the Shepherd's song is the simplicity of the natural, where in 'Nonne monstrum' it is the simplicity of the artificial: the true against the false.

The formal construction of the scene calls for an element of reprise after 'Nonne monstrum', over and above the da capo or refrain aspect of each separate piece, and this is supplied by a repeat of the Messenger's song, recast as a duet for the Messenger and the Shepherd. But strict formality would have been out of place in a drama proceeding so swiftly to its climax; and the music is significantly varied to meet the new needs of the situation, which are, broadly, that Oedipus's self-delusion, having nearly destroyed the vestiges of nobility in his character, must be quickly and decisively swept away. The text thus summarises the position: Oedipus was found on the mountain, abandoned by his parents, Laius and Jocasta; he killed his father and married his mother; would that these things could be left unsaid.[39] The music meanwhile reverts emphatically to the Messenger's 'earth language', uttered firmly but softly, as if with reluctance but under divine compulsion. These things must, human sympathy notwithstanding, be made known. The voices sing partly in unison, partly in a form of close-knit two-part counterpoint, and the music's rhetoric is intensified by changes of harmony and orchestration. Previously in a free Dorian G minor but over a dominant (D) pedal, it now adopts a pure Dorian D minor over a tonic (D) pedal, with hard articulation (of the pedal notes especially) by trombone and timpani in place of the original discreet string support. The higher pitch of the top line (D instead of G) sharpens the sense of finality, and this is clinched in the middle section, the enunciation of the charge against Oedipus, where the two voices sing this note in unison, echoed by the choral tenors. D remains the crucial note – the note of judgement – right to the end of the scene.

One other crucial piece of imagery lends a sense of oracular fatalism to the climax of this scene. The listener perhaps does not notice that the motivic rhythm of the Messenger's 'Reppereram' at fig. 139 is that of the word 'trivium', repeated menacingly by the chorus just before Oedipus's 'confession' in the previous scene (see above, Ex. 10).[40] But in this final, summatory section, it becomes as nearly explicit as makes no difference. At fig. 161, two clarinets, *sforzando*, turn it into a five-note pulsation in demisemiquavers; next at 163 the strings, without voices, play both the three-note and five-note versions as semiquavers on a plain D minor chord, later adapting them to accompany the closing vocal phrase at 166. The pulsated version is then carried over into the coda, in both its semiquaver and demisemiquaver forms, accompanying Oedipus's final acknowledgement of his guilt. Thus the turning-point in Oedipus's life becomes a muffled drumbeat for his downfall (Ex. 15).

But Stravinsky evades the issue, at this point, of a tonally decisive judgement on Oedipus, aware perhaps of the danger of banality lurking in so candidly nineteenth-century a device. At the start of the coda, the 'trivium' pulsations seem to alternate D minor and major (F versus F#), and the final chord is apparently D major, though the context leaves some doubt about it. For in reality the 'D major' chords of the opening are B minor, as is shown by the absence of the note A and the late addition of the root B on the timpani each time the 'major' chord sounds. Oedipus's vocal line is entirely in B minor, though laid out in such a way as to avoid bitonal clashes with the D minor string pulsation. Yet the D minor/major ambiguity is genuine enough, and survives in the final chord, which contains neither A nor B but is firmly bedded on the root D (Ex. 16).

Throughout his neo-classical period Stravinsky was fond of these ambiguities: between keys a third apart, created by the omission of chord roots, and between major and minor modes on the one tonic. Yet here in *Oedipus rex* the device is unexpected. Why invent an ambiguity to express a certainty as divinely inspired as Oedipus's 'Lux facta est'? The answer must surely be that there is not so much an ambiguity as an enrichment, an opening out of possibilities. We saw how Oedipus's final aria 'Nonne monstrum' portrayed his inner collapse through the reduction of a conventional language to a

Ex. 15(a) p. 76

Ex. 15(b) p. 77

Ex. 15(c) p. 79

Ex. 16 p. 79

meaningless routine. Clearly the entry of light into that benighted soul called for some fresh musical initiative, and Stravinsky, typically, found one that is rich but lucid, direct but resonant.

The cord and the clasp

As the final D major fades away, the Messenger, who has withdrawn with the Shepherd during Oedipus's 'Natus sum quo nefastum est', reappears. But, like Jocasta at her first entrance (and perhaps for the same reason), he is made to wait before he speaks. 'I like', says Stravinsky in *Dialogues* (p. 29), 'to acknowledge that the Queen Mother must have a lot to say by giving [the audience] a pause before she says it.' How much more the Messenger who heralds her death. In fact it is the Speaker who now steps forward, announces what, to the composer's own later irritation, he calls the 'famous monologue: The Divine Jocasta is Dead', and describes summarily Jocasta's suicide by hanging, Oedipus's self-blinding with the pin of her golden clasp, and his gentle expulsion from Thebes. This final narration interweaves with phrases of the fanfare. And only then does the Messenger attempt the 'famous monologue'.

Stravinsky's complaint against this episode was that there is supposedly no monologue, only what he wittily but unfairly called 'a four-word singing telegram' ('Divum Jocastae caput mortuum').[41] But the point is that, as the Speaker explains, the Messenger can hardly speak for emotion, and 'the chorus takes his part and helps him . . .'. So what in Sophocles is a monologue becomes, in Stravinsky, a series of choruses with the Messenger's lapidary announcement as a refrain, thrice repeated. It hardly takes a musical detective to suggest that what in fact happened is that Stravinsky decided, for dramatic

63

and structural reasons, to make this final scene into a large-scale chorus, leaving Cocteau with the problem of how to present the monologue, whose text after all is retained, and in a form which does, technically, *remain* monologue. His solution – to, as it were, trail the monologue by title – may strike us now as a piece of snobbish obscurantism. But it is not out of keeping with the oblique tendency of the entire narration, with its deliberate ellipses and omissions. And it lends suitable verbal weight to a moment for which, after all, the composer decided fanfares were an appropriate kind of music.[42]

The choral ending is manifestly that of an oratorio. Tragic operas (at least in the Italian tradition on which Stravinsky chiefly drew) seldom end chorally, while the choral endings of eighteenth-century operas on tragic subjects are typically associated with a *deus ex machina* and attendant jollifications. But Stravinsky will also not have overlooked the play's own choral ending, which Cocteau retained from first to last. In Sophocles, the final chorus is brief and moralistic, with the trenchant conclusion, 'Count no man happy until he has ended his life free of pain.' In Greek drama generally, the chorus does not only or even chiefly narrate, but acts as a kind of prompt for narration, urging other characters to tell what they know, adopting the role of innocent bystander, and also expressing broad responses, often of a pious or philosophical kind. In his original text, Cocteau retained these functions, but with some added emphasis on the chorus's role as men of Thebes, intimately involved in the tragedy. For instance, he allocated to the chorus the Priest's part in the opening scene, and he sneaked into the closing speech the important words 'on l'aimait' ('he was loved' or, possibly, 'we loved him'), which, in Daniélou's Latin, became 'te amabam' ('I loved you'). Stravinsky objected later to what he saw as 'a journalist's caption and a blot of sentimentality wholly alien to the manners of the work'. But in Sophocles this tone of almost personal loss is ever-present in the choral writing, though it looms less large in Cocteau's text. What may strike us as more surprising is that neither author saw fit to retain Sophocles's moral, so apt, one might have thought, to choral setting, in the Faustian vein of Beethoven, Liszt and Mahler.[43]

The closest textual parallels to Cocteau's ending in modern western music are the pietistic final choruses in Bach's passion settings: 'We sit down tearfully and call to you in the grave' (St Matthew) and 'Rest well, ye holy limbs which I no longer mourn' (St John). But though there certainly is a resemblance between the roles of the choruses in Sophocles and Bach, it seems to have had no specifically musical influence on Stravinsky at this stage. The Messenger's announcement, which is in essentials musically identical the four times he makes it, does have a quasi-religious, incantatory tone, but it is that of a responsory, with the Messenger in the role of cantor. It differs obviously from that model in the frenzied character of the choral 'responses', but also in the fact that repetition is more usually a property of the response than of the intonation. All the same, there is corroboration that Stravinsky was thinking religion at this point, in the fact that the Messenger's music is based entirely on the octatonic scale, and moreover on a form of that scale which, in his neo-classical phase, Stravinsky usually afterwards reserved for sacred music or music where he was apparently feeling particularly Russian (often much the same thing in his case). In general, the octatonic scale is not particularly prominent in *Oedipus rex*,[44] and it is nearly absent from his next work, *Apollo*. But it comes back with a vengeance in the *Symphony of Psalms* (1930), Stravinsky's first candidly sacred work of any size.

But if the Messenger in some ways resembles a priest, the resemblance remains essentially operatic. The situation is ritualised but theatrical. The 'priest' intones his words four times, as if to the four corners of the kingdom. But the atmosphere is one of terror and theatrically real catastrophe, not the commemorative or prophylactic disaster of the Stations of the Cross or the Burial Service. Whether or not Stravinsky saw *Turandot* in Milan in May 1926, the parallels between this final scene of *Oedipus rex* and the riddle scene of Puccini's last opera are interesting, especially between the Messenger's music and the Unknown Prince's answers to the three riddles (as well as his earlier thrice-repeated demand to the Emperor to be allowed to undergo the trial). The similarity is both musical and rhetorical; the two scenes have the same kind of formalised barbarity, the invocatory 'pitch' of the repeated incantations is similar, and the pacing of the music, as well as some of its detailing, is comparable.[45] Puccini, of course, was himself by this time under Stravinsky's stylistic influence. But the resemblance in the present case is less of style than of dramatic gesture, backed up by some musical detail. In fact it is the gestural similarity which suggests that Stravinsky may have been affected by Puccini, since it is mainly at this level, too, that the influence of Verdi operated on him.

To achieve his choral ending, Stravinsky greatly compressed the action of the original play. Creon does not reappear, and there is no mention of Oedipus's daughters, Antigone and Ismene, nor of his wish to take them with him (Oedipus himself does not sing). In place of this potentially diffuse and distracting episode, the composer devised a brilliantly concise and overwhelmingly powerful climax, in which the choral 'responses' to the Messenger's exclamations grow in intensity until they implode in the music which opened the work. These four successive sections (as ever, for male voices only) contain some of the most vigorous and original choral writing by any twentieth-century composer – a marvellous preparation for the *Symphony of Psalms* three years later. Oddly enough, the source of their energy seems to lie, as Stravinsky himself was the first to point out,[46] in precisely that regularity of metre which, for him, was such a novel feature of the work. The hectic trochees of 'Mulier in vestibulo' pound along like some terrifying infernal march, their regularity if anything emphasised by the thrown verbal accents ('ĭn vēstĭbūlŏ, ĭn vĕstībŭlō') and distraught word repetitions ('ēt pŭlsārĕ, ēt pŭlsārĕ, pū 'lsārĕ, ēt ˇŌedĭpūs pŭlsārĕ, pū 'lsārĕ). Throughout, the chorus's 6/8 dotted crotchet equals the Messenger's 3/4 crotchet, so that the pulse is always maintained, even while the terror freezes, as it were, at every repeat of 'Divum Jocastae caput mortuum'. At the 'Aspikite' fugato (fig. 192), the 6/8 quaver (=396) becomes a 2/4 semiquaver, introducing a new kind of headlong movement, though still within the metric scheme, which finally breaks down only at the return to the music of the opening scene. This whole sequence is superbly conceived in terms of the stage. At 'Aspikite' the chorus, which has so far been describing the unseen circumstances of Jocasta's death and Oedipus's self-blinding, glimpses Oedipus himself for the first time, though the audience does not yet see him; and the subtle change of pace prepares us for the horrific sight the chorus has been telling us to expect. Then, as the Messenger for the last time repeats his announcement of *Jocasta's* death, Oedipus himself appears, and the music finally climaxes on the tonic major of the key that has dominated Act II, G minor – the key of Jocasta's and the Messenger's arias and, as we shall shortly discover, the key of the work's ending. This major chord strikingly varies the original opening gesture (B♭ minor), suggesting not triumph, of course, but fulfilment: the ultimate vindication of the prophecy. At first G major masquerades as the dominant of C major, in which key the chorus briefly reverts to fugato as a musical correlative for the idea of Oedipus showing himself to the people ('Aspikite' – 'observe'; 'Ellum, regem Oedipoda' – 'Behold, King Oedipus'), before settling into G minor for the last farewell, to the oscillating quaver thirds with which this same chorus implored the king's rescue from the plague.

He has not, after all, let them down. There will be no more plague. If the irony of this musical reminder has no exact equivalent in Sophocles, it is perhaps only because words cannot, without gaucheness, make so complex a point so economically or with such emotional force. Nevertheless Creon's *obiter dictum*, taken over by Cocteau in the play text but not the opera, has some equivalent force. 'Do not seek to be master in everything, for the things you mastered did not follow you throughout your life.'

4

How it all came to be known

To turn from the external politics of the creation of *Oedipus rex* to the actual process of composition as shown by the composer's sketches and drafts is to follow Plato from the superficial world of shadow and illusion into the deeper reality of ultimate forms. This is a familiar experience to students of Stravinsky's sketchbooks. They reveal a mentality completely absorbed by the act of discovery, as described so vividly, a few years later, in the third Harvard lecture: 'we grub about in expectation of our pleasure, guided by our scent, and suddenly we stumble against an unknown obstacle. It gives us a jolt, a shock, and this shock fecundates our creative power.'[1] Stravinsky nearly always grubbed at the piano, but whenever he encountered 'something unexpected', he would write it down.[2]

The sketches are thus a record not so much of arduous labour, as with Beethoven or Mahler, as of moments of recognition or, to use Stravinsky's own term, 'observation'. Page by page, the work in hand materialises on paper in the form of precise musical images that differ little in essence from their appearance in the finished score. Hardly anything goes unused. Once notated, an idea will be refined in various ways. From time to time, its elements may be arranged in slightly altered sequence; barring, articulation, verbal underlay and other secondary details may well be modified or added, melodic intervals may change. But the identity between sketch and fair copy is nearly always unmistakable in respect of those elements by which we normally recognise a piece of music: rhythm, melodic shape, harmony. This crystallisation of musical images is then followed swiftly by one or more formal drafts in which the continuity of the whole section is established. Wrong turnings are soon corrected by alternative drafts which, as often as not, effectively settle the eventual form. So sure-handed is this process that the reader has a distinct impression that the full draft is no more than a 'realisation' of a temporality latent in the original images. There is relatively little struggle, and Stravinsky rarely proceeds to a new section before the essential form and most of the detail of its predecessor have been fixed in short score.

In most of these respects, the sketches for *Oedipus rex* are very little different from those for *The Rite of Spring*. Certainly there is no change of method to accommodate the particular continuities, such as they may be, of a neo-tonal, neo-formalistic, neo-classical manner. The fact that *Oedipus rex* was apparently composed more or less in score-order, as far as its broad sequence goes, is not particularly significant, since the internal sub-sections of each 'scene' were not. Stravinsky's first annotations for the opening, for instance, were for the ostinato passage between figs. 2 and 7, after which he composed Oedipus's 'Liberi, vos liberabo' solo (11/12 January 1926), then the transition that precedes it (figs 14–16: 13 January), then – with more apparent difficulty – the preceding music back to fig. 10. By the time he left Nice for Paris on 19 or 20 January, he had drafted most of the music between figs. 10 and 19 but had barely so much as sketched the very start of the work. This opening music, together with the ostinato chorus at fig. 2, was eventually composed (though not immediately) on his return from Paris on the 25th. But the rest of the first scene, from figs. 19 to 27, had to wait until his return from an extensive conducting tour towards the end of March, at which point he composed the 'Quid fakiendum' chorus (fig. 21) and Oedipus's 'Uxoris frater' solo, followed by the preceding chorus 'Serva nos adhuc' (which adapts earlier music), and finally the choral welcome to Creon at fig. 25.

Admittedly, this apparently random sequence of composition is somewhat exceptional and may be connected with some problem to do with the Latin text. It was on 19 January that Cocteau wrote to his mother complaining of having to 'begin my work all over again',[3] and since this was probably the very day of Stravinsky's departure for Paris, it looks as if the composer contacted the librettist that day or the day before with a request for a textual revision of the opening (hence perhaps Cocteau's 'begin'). Stravinsky certainly already possessed the elements of the Latin text for the first scene, since it largely figures in the January sketches. But it is noticeable that the words which were eventually to open the work, 'Kaedit nos pestis', appear first (14 January) to what became a purely instrumental idea (bassoon and horn at fig. 11), a misapplication which suggests that Stravinsky had at that stage no clear mental image of how the work would actually begin, though fragmentary notations for the start do appear – to these same words – soon afterwards (15 and 17 January).[4]

Several other details of the opening scene were eventually relocated or modified, in ways that are characteristic of Stravinsky's general working method. For example, the first notation for Oedipus's first aria, 'Liberi, vos liberabo', sets the phrase 'Liberabo vos' almost exactly as at fig. 16/5 but at the pitch and with the interval sequence later used for 'oraculum consulit' in the second aria (at fig. 23/3). Evidently this figure was Stravinsky's primary musical image of Oedipus in his pride and self-confidence. But it was an image conceived independently of a precise context. On the very same page of the Basel sketchbook, the composer noted the other characteristic figure of the 'Liberi' aria, the setting of the phrase 'Eg' Oedipus vos diligo'. This was formulated not in its initial shape (fig. 18), but in its subsequent shape as at fig. 18/3. There follows a draft of the complete aria, which Stravinsky seems then to have transferred, more fully worked, into the Washington manuscript, where – similarly – it occupies the opening recto pages. But Stravinsky continued to work on the exact setting of 'Eg' Oedipus', eventually arriving at the final form at about the sixth attempt. Yet the first notation had already hit off the idea quite accurately. It looks as if Stravinsky became uncertain about the relationship of duplets and triplets in this figure, and the exact role of the syncopated quaver. At first he tried to get the rhythm he wanted without bothering about the metre – a method which harks back to works like *The Rite of Spring*, where the metre was usually a function of the rhythmic groupings. Then he tried respecting the metre by abandoning the triplet. In the end he kept the triplet within a regular metre, while using the syncopation, and a changing stress on the word 'vos', to blur the conventional accents.

Notwithstanding the need to experiment with figures of this kind (and despite outside distractions), he seems to have maintained an impressively even work-rate throughout the composition. He was never a rapid or fluent composer. But nor was he often held up by intractable creative or technical difficulties. Section by section, the music emerges steadily, reliably and with hardly any waste. The Basel sketchbook records the completion of the work in draft form on 14 March 1927, on which day Stravinsky wrote to Ernest Ansermet that he was embarking on the orchestral score: 'I've been very annoyed by all these people who cling to this Oedipus, even though it is none of their business, and even though its meaning escapes them as completely as it will certainly escape them in the future. Never mind – I work and stop thinking about it. All the while I pray God to keep me from these people, and that makes me calmer.'[5] Orchestration of the first act was completed by 30 March, and of the whole score by 10 May. Stravinsky seems to have gone directly from the (Washington) draft vocal score to the fair-copy full score (also now in the Library of Congress) – a remarkable fact if true, as this was the first time he had written for a standard symphony orchestra since completing *The Nightingale* in 1914.[6] A few orchestral sketches (dated, at the end, 28 March) complete the Basel sketch-book, and there are also some loose leaves. But the manuscript orchestral score is itself essentially clean.

Oedipus confronts his public

Stravinsky himself accompanied the avant-première at the house of the Princesse Edmond de Polignac on 29 May,[7] and also conducted the first public performance, at the Théâtre Sarah-Bernhardt in Paris, on 30 May. The cast was: Stéphane Belina-Skupievsky (Oedipus), Hélène Sadoven (Jocasta), Georges Lanskoy (Creon/Messenger), Kapiton Zaporojetz (Tiresias), Michel D'Arial (Shepherd), and Pierre Brasseur (Speaker). Cocteau had certainly assumed that he would himself take the part of the Speaker.[8] But, according to Stravinsky, Diaghilev chose the 'very handsome, very young' Brasseur 'deliberately . . . to spite Cocteau'.[9] So Cocteau was in the audience for the first performance, sitting next to Klemperer, to whom he at one point whispered (referring to Stravinsky's conducting): 'He can't do it. This is impossible.'[10]

Amid the delights of the Ballets Russes season, which included the young Serge Lifar in Sauguet's *La Chatte* (with choreography by Balanchine and constructivist designs by Naum Gabo and Antoine Pevsner), the new Prokofiev ballet *Le Pas d'acier*, and several colourful revivals, the austere *Oedipus rex* – unstaged except for long black drapes with the men of the chorus 'sombrement vêtus'[11] – cut little ice. The press did not hasten to review it, and their tone when they did so was no more than respectful, with the distinguished exception of Boris de Schloezer, who saw at once the power and originality of the score, while rejecting the device of the Speaker.[12] De Schloezer refers to the 'conditions déplorables' of the first performance, which is probably a tactful reference to Stravinsky's poor conducting. In a footnote to Vera Sudeikina's published diaries, Robert Craft hints that her failure to comment on the performance was because she did not at the time want to write anything that she could not show to Stravinsky: 'She used to describe the first performance of *Oedipus* in considerable detail, as well as Stravinsky's foul mood following the poor audience reception of the work.'[13] Certainly, Stravinsky was as yet inexperienced as a conductor, and while *Oedipus* is a less difficult score than *The Rite of Spring*, it is hard to imagine the future perpetrator of the dreadful 1929 Columbia recording of that ballet achieving more than passable results with this new, unfamiliar, and possibly under-rehearsed opera-oratorio.

Stravinsky conducted the work again in Amsterdam just under a year after the Paris première, on 24 April 1928, again in concert form but with better performers and much greater success.[14] By that time, however, it had been staged at least twice, possibly three times. The stage première in Vienna, conducted by Franz Schalk[15] on 23 February 1928, is sketchily documented, partly because the Viennese critics (like their German colleagues) took the music so seriously that they left themselves hardly any space to discuss matters of production or design. The Staatsoper producer abandoned the idea of a statuesque chorus, and instead put the choir in the pit while having the stage chorus mimed by stand-ins dressed as greybeards ('Mummelgreise'). He also, according to the *Zeitschrift für Musik* reviewer Emil Petschnig, substituted effects of lighting and colour for the more solid décor outlined in the score.[16] But the Speaker duly appeared in a *Frack* (evening-dress suit), as specified. Stravinsky did not attend the Vienna performances, and seems indeed to have forgotten about them.[17] He was at that time in Berlin for rehearsals of the Kroll Opera production under Klemperer, which opened two nights later, on the 25th, in a triple-bill with *Mavra* and *Petrushka*.

Thanks partly to the composer's own participation, partly to the notoriety of the Kroll itself, we know more about the Berlin production. Ewald Dülberg's functional, rectilinear set, while devoid of classical associations, seems to have answered the element of conscious objectivity in the music, and was later much imitated in German productions of *Oedipus*.[18] To judge from contemporary notices, Klemperer's staging was reasonably faithful to the preface and stage directions, with the important and striking exception that the Speaker was not allowed to wear evening dress and appeared instead in what Stravinsky remembered as a 'black pierrot costume' but the *ZfM* reviewer Adolf Diesterweg described as a 'zeitlose [timeless] Kostüm'.[19] Stravinsky reported being told by the 'director' (presumably the Intendant Tietjen) that 'in our country only the *Kapellmeister* is allowed to wear a *Frack*'. But Diesterweg suggested that Klemperer allowed the change because he was 'nervous that the up-to-date appearance of this Baedeker of the stage would provoke merriment in the audience', which, on the first night, was dominated by a block-booking of the Berlin Chamber of Commerce (Verein Berliner Kaufleute und Industrieller), though it also contained some distinguished individuals, including Schoenberg and – according to Stravinsky – Hindemith, Einstein and Hofmannsthal, himself the author of an elaborate adaptation of Sophocles's play (*Ödipus und die Sphinx*, 1906).[20]

Several other German houses put *Oedipus* on during 1928, including Düsseldorf (where the set seems broadly to have echoed the score preface, but the singers wore no masks), Essen, Magdeburg and Mainz.[21] Essen saw the piece again, in a fresh production, in 1930. Such commitment to a work which might have been expected to arouse, at best, ambivalence among the more earnest Teutonic critics reflected Stravinsky's overwhelming reputation in Germany in the late twenties. He was well-known there, and invariably fêted, as a pianist and (in due course) as a conductor; but his own music was also hugely admired and his new works invariably treated with respect. The German reviews of *Oedipus*, for example, show that – even where this or that detail of style or presentation may have raised an eyebrow – Stravinsky was essentially regarded as above reproach. This is in refreshing contrast to his French (not to mention British) press of those years, where pedantic point-scoring and flippant *espièglerie* were the order of the day. The French took years to appreciate the profound seriousness of Stravinsky's art, through all its superficial changes of style. But with the Germans it was its seriousness which struck home immediately, and set it clearly above the merely shocking manifestations of so much other new music of the twenties, whether from France or Germany.

Unfortunately for Stravinsky, money and politics soon combined to drive his music out of Germany and Austria altogether, and the 1930 Essen *Oedipus* may well have been the last new staging in either land until the fifties. But few other countries possessed the operatic resources – or, one might add, gumption – to stage new works with any frequency; and *Oedipus* had the extra disadvantage that hard-pressed theatre managements could look at its subtitle, 'opera-oratorio', and persuade themselves that in any case it was not really a stage work at all. The Leningrad performances under Klimov in spring 1928 (as well as Ansermet's performance there the following season) were in concert. In Italy, *Oedipus* seems to have been staged only once before the war, in Florence in May 1937, and in Switzerland also once, in Zurich in 1934.[22] But in England and France it fared even less well. Paris had to wait a quarter-century for its stage première in 1952; yet even this was not a full stage production, but an oratorio performance accompanying a series of *tableaux vivants*. The British stage première was at the Edinburgh Festival in August 1956, in a performance by the visiting Hamburg State Opera; the first native production was at Sadlers Wells in 1960. Until then it was more or less routine in London, the oratorio capital of the universe, to count *Oedipus* as an oratorio and to perform it as such. It was a concert performance which the young Benjamin Britten heard and praised at the Queen's Hall in February 1936.[23] But Britten's vigorous response to this latest phase of Stravinsky's work was unusual in the intellectual swamp of contemporary British music criticism.

When an overpowering figure like Ernest Newman could so abandon simple logic as to assert that 'much of the music is insignificant. Yet as a whole it leaves us decidedly impressed . . .', it is hardly surprising to find the less weighty Herbert Hughes predicting, from the score, that 'while pretending to be tragedy, [the work will have] all the authentic cerebrations of jazz'.[24] On the whole Stravinsky's London press of the twenties and thirties has a persistent and depressing 'what can you expect of foreigners' air, in sharp contrast to the composer's experience with British singers and orchestral players, whom he regarded as among the most competent, assiduous and impartial in the world.[25]

One other pre-war production deserves mention, that of the American stage première conducted by Leopold Stokowski at the New York Met on 21 April 1931.[26] The designer, Robert Edmond Jones, abandoned the idea of masked, immobile singers, and instead produced a cast of huge, nine-foot tall puppets, 'towering figures, frugal and angular of gesture, gravely composed and rather sorrowful of mien, symbolizing the persons of the tragic play'.[27] The solo singers themselves remained unseen, as did the Speaker (Wayland Rudd), who enunciated the text through loudspeakers. But the chorus, 'blue-robed, sat in serried ranks on the stage, which was shrouded in shadow'.[28] This impressive idea seems not to have borne fruit in practice. Gilman found the puppets' gestures 'stiff and limited . . . , suggestive of embarrassed semaphores at a costume party', while for Downes 'the puppets fell between two extremes, being neither completely classic nor completely fantastical'. But it should be noted that Stravinsky knew about this production, even if he never saw it, and he approved its ruling idea. The notion of puppets, he said in *Dialogues* (p. 24), 'did occur to me, in fact, and I had been impressed by Gordon Craig's puppets when he showed them to me in Rome in 1917. But I am also fond of masks . . .' Probably Stravinsky's final instinct was that the tension between the rigidity of masks and the humanity of their wearers would be more impressive than the mechanised fatalism of even the most brilliantly executed puppets. If so, he might have agreed with Craig's idea of the 'Über-Marionette' as 'the actor plus fire, minus egoism, the fire of the gods and demons, without the smoke and steam of mortality'.[29]

Since the war, *Oedipus rex* has become an operatic repertory piece, and a comprehensive survey of productions would be both repetitive and, for the most part, unilluminating, since it seems that few producers have seriously broken with the work's rigorously prescribed gestural and dramaturgical style. The main tendency, perhaps predictably, has been for the Speaker to invade the action to a greater or lesser degree, as he did in Lars Runsten's Copenhagen production of November 1967 and in Patrick Libby's staging for English National Opera North at Leeds in March 1981. Stravinsky's view of such liberties may be guessed in view of his general attitude to the role of the Speaker. His own favourite among the few stagings he would admit to having seen was the *tableaux vivants* production designed by Cocteau for the Festival de l'oeuvre du XX siècle at the Théâtre des Champs-Élysées in Paris in May 1952.[30] This may seem surprising, since the seven mimed tableaux appear to have had only a passing connection with the action of the opera. They showed: the arrival of the plague at Thebes; the sorrow of Athene, 'sauterelle de l'été grec'; the Oracles (with Tiresias questioned by Oedipus and Jocasta together); the Sphinx; the Oedipus complex; Jocasta thrice dead – as mother, wife and queen; and the blind Oedipus with his daughters and the chorus. But Stravinsky was impressed above all by Cocteau's masks, and, 'though it contradicted my idea, . . . his use of symbolic mime'.[31] Cocteau himself took the part of the Speaker on this occasion, as he had done in Stravinsky's recording with the Cologne Radio the previous autumn, and as he was to do years later in a famous late-night concert with the composer in London's Royal Festival Hall, in November 1959.[32] But though Cocteau's delivery of the text on these recordings is as sharp and unforgiving as a dentist's drill, it seems not to have reconciled Stravinsky to the device.[33] In the very same month as the 1952 Paris production, he conducted a concert performance in Brussels without a speaker.[34] And he presumably did the same at the Venice Biennale in 1958 (at the time of the première of *Threni*), when Vittorio de Sica proved unavailable to take the part.

A perhaps more intriguing question is how far Stravinsky achieved the vocal qualities he sought in any of his own performances. The part of Oedipus himself 'should not be sung by a large operatic voice, but by a lyrical one'.[35] But of the tenors in his recordings, only Léopold Simoneau, in the Paris recording, really fulfils this prescription. Simoneau, a Mozart specialist (and a well-known Rakewell in *The Rake's Progress*), was unusual in being able to combine clarity and fluency in melisma with a certain force of dramatic penetration. But the part was for a long time more often taken by dramatic tenors, like Ronald Dowd, or even Wagner tenors, like Helmut Melchert, who sang in the 1959 London performance. In practice, Stravinsky was for obvious reasons happy if he could find a tenor with the artistry to dispatch the part accurately and with intelligent musicianship, which is no doubt why he went to some lengths to secure the services of Peter Pears on several occasions in the 1950s, even though Pears's highly individual voice can hardly have been what he had in mind when writing the part, and is certainly far from the *bel canto* quality mentioned as desirable by Britten in his review of the London première.

Stravinsky left descriptions of all the other vocal types in *Oedipus rex* except Jocasta. The Shepherd, he said, is a *tenore di grazia*, Tiresias a *basso profundo*, and Creon (and thus by implication the Messenger) a *basso cantante*.[36] These descriptions are, of course, to some extent character designations as well as trademarks. Tiresias has to be profound as well as deep-voiced; Creon has to sound simple and uncomplicated; the Shepherd needs to display a certain airy detachment. But since the music for these roles, unlike for Oedipus, does not really change in the course of the work, the qualities are simply a matter of type-casting. Jocasta is another matter. Described in the score as a mezzo-soprano, she needs the dark colouring and strong chest register associated with that voice, but must also be extremely agile to make anything of the patter music in her duet with Oedipus. A strong Verdi mezzo is clearly called for, such as Shirley Verrett (on Stravinsky's 1962 CBS recording) or a natural Carmen like Tatyana Troyanos (in the recording by Leonard Bernstein), and emphatically not the old-fashioned wobbly contralto such as Stravinsky was too often saddled with in his other recordings. Jocasta may be a grandmother, but senior citizen in the modern welfare-state sense clearly she is not. Her poise and dignity must be paramount, since they are her version of Oedipus's smug self-esteem which is so shattered when the truth comes out.

Revised and revisited

In October 1947, Stravinsky informed his new publisher Ralph Hawkes that 'I airmailed you today my vocal score [of *Oedipus rex*] with many red-ink corrections and alterations quite sufficient to obtain a new copyright.'[37] It is a common fallacy about Stravinsky's revisions that they were carried out solely for reasons of copyright, though this certainly was one motive, just as his later donation of manuscripts to the Library of Congress was partly prompted by a desire to take advantage of the US law that permitted artists to deduct from their taxable income the nominal value of art works donated to public collections. The point is that Stravinsky was by nature a reviser, and many of the alterations later incorporated in newly copyrighted scores were entered on the manuscript or printed first editions long before there was any question of such copyright.[38] Of *Oedipus rex*, for instance, he claimed in *Dialogues* (p. 29) that 'the revisions are not mere copyright changes, but improvements instituted in my manuscript immediately following the first performance.' No doubt there is some author's licence in this remark. Immediate changes to the vocal score could surely have been entered on the proofs of the first edition, which only came out in about December 1927. But changes in orchestration were another matter, since it appears that the 1927 full score was never actually published.[39]

Above all, the many new hard articulations in the 1947 revision were probably omitted from the first edition simply because their inclusion was not thought necessary and because it was in Stravinsky's nature in the twenties to produce an unnuanced score. They may have been added to the score in 1947 as copyright changes, but that does not mean they were musical changes in any practical sense. No doubt, *mutatis mutandis*, Stravinsky had always performed the work in that way. He did not establish a new articulative character by substantial rescoring, as he had done with *Petrushka* and proceeded to do with the *Symphonies of wind instruments*. In fact the significant orchestral changes in the revised *Oedipus* are relatively few, and usually either support the voice (like the added trumpet obbligato in 'Nonne monstrum') or make it easier to hear, like the simplified bass scoring at fig. 12/3. There are the usual rebarrings, though many fewer than in the metrically more complicated earlier works. Rhythmic changes are usually purely notational or else designed to sharpen articulation, like the change from triplets to semiquavers in the strings at fig. 129. Changes of musical substance are minimal. Most striking is Oedipus's entry on 'Invidia fortunam odit', which in the revised score cuts in on Tiresias in such a way that the tenor entry is imperceptible as it tries to call in question the certainty of the old man's prophecy. The one other significant compositional change is the addition of sectional repeats in Jocasta's aria and the following duet. But after conducting *Oedipus* in the Toronto concert of May 1967 in which the composer himself conducted in public for the last time, Craft noted in his diary that 'tonight's performance convinces me that the repeats . . . , both added in 1949 [sic], are miscalculations'. [40]

Another remark on the same diary page gives the reader pause. 'I.S. denies that [Oedipus] is so very different from his earlier theater works with voice. "The singers are in the pit and the dancers on the stage in *Renard*, *Les Noces*, *Pulcinella* as well, and the title part in *The Nightingale* should be performed in the same way."' Does this mean that the procedures adopted in Paris in 1927 (soloists in the pit), Vienna in 1928 (chorus in the pit, mimes on stage) and New York in 1931 (soloists out of sight, puppets on stage), specifically reflected his intentions, or was he merely referring to the general concept of dissociation involved in the use of masks, a tableau-like action, and a narrator? Had his views on the staging of *Oedipus* changed? It seems unlikely, even though his own favourite staging had similarly been one in which the stage action was mimed; his parenthetic comment on the 1952 semi-staging in *Dialogues* (p. 25) – 'it contradicted my idea' – needs to be borne in mind. If we take such remarks too literally we shall probably conclude that Stravinsky ended up thinking of *Oedipus rex* as an oratorio/concert-work after all: 'The music is more important than the action, as the words were more important than the action in Shakespeare.'[41] Yes, but even so nobody would think of playing Shakespeare in concert form.

The fact is that Stravinsky was given to self-contradiction, apparently arbitrary changes of mind and, occasionally, deliberate obfuscations. Those who persist in seeing him as the supreme apostle of the rational and the self-consistent in music miss the point completely. Take his attitude to the reprise of the 'Gloria' chorus at the start of Act II. In all editions of the score, the sequence is: (a) Gloria ends Act I – (b) curtain falls – (c) curtain rises (Act II) – (d) reprise of Gloria – (e) Speaker – (f) Jocasta's aria. But not once in his four recorded performances does Stravinsky follow this sequence. The 1951 and 1959 recordings, both based on or taken from concert performances, omit (d) (the Gloria reprise), and presumably also any equivalent of (b) and (c).[42] The 1952 *tableaux-vivants* performance seems also to have been given as a single unbroken act, and again there is no Gloria reprise. But in his later studio recording with the Opera Society of Washington (1962), Stravinsky makes the Gloria reprise *after* the Speaker's introduction, a sequence which accords with his more or less contemporary remark in *Dialogues* (p. 29) that 'I repeat the "*Gloria*" chorus after the narrator's speech . . . because I prefer to go directly, without narration, from *tutti* G major to *solo* flute and harp G minor.' He could have added that to follow the Speaker's grim warning about the word 'Trivium' with a brilliant chorus in praise of the very queen who will shortly, unwittingly, reveal her own and Oedipus's doom is a stroke of dramatic irony worthy of Sophocles, whereas repeating the chorus before the Speaker is a mere slavish echo of Cocteau's time-distorting idea in *Orphée*. Yet at the Toronto concert of May 1967 Stravinsky asked Robert Craft 'to repeat the *Gloria* before the Speaker, as in the original score'.[43]

These vacillations, however, are untypical of Stravinsky's attitude to the score of *Oedipus*, and merely reflect a certain impatience with those conditions of theatrical performance over which he had limited control but which he knew he could not escape because his genius was so quintessentially theatrical. In terms of the musical text – whether as printed or as performed – *Oedipus rex* was one of the major works that seem to have given him least anxiety. Certainly his recorded performances differ little in their general musical character, just as his printed texts for the most part vary only in secondary or notational details. It would be good to have on record an early performance, like the 1928 London broadcast. But one feels it would only confirm what we know already: that the conception changed less than the technical means for realising it.

Appendix A

The libretto

PROLOGUE

LE SPEAKER

Spectateurs,

Vous allez entendre une version
latine d'Œdipe-Roi.

Afin de vous épargner tout effort
d'oreilles et de mémoire et comme
l'opéra-oratorio ne conserve des
scènes qu'un certain aspect monumental, je vous rappellerai, au fur
et à mesure, le drame de Sophocle.

Sans le savoir, Œdipe est aux
prises avec les forces qui nous
surveillent de l'autre côté de la
mort. Elles lui tendent, depuis sa
naissance, un piège que vous allez
voir se fermer là.

Voici le drame:

Thèbes se démoralise. Après le
Sphinx, la peste. Le chœur supplie
Œdipe de sauver sa ville. Œdipe a
vaincu le Sphinx; il promet. (*exit*)

Après le Prologue, rideau.
En scène: Œdipe, Le Chœur

CHORUS

Kædit nos pestis,
Theba peste moritur.
E peste serva nos

SPEAKER

Ladies and Gentlemen,

You are about to hear a Latin
version of King Oedipus.

In order to spare you all effort
of ear and memory and as the opera-
oratorio preserves only a certain
monumental aspect of the play, I
shall recall Sophocles's drama as
we go along.

Without knowing it, Oedipus is in
the grip of those forces which keep
watch on us from beyond death. When
he was born, they set him a trap
which you will see close here.

This is the plot:

Thebes is prostrate. After the
Sphinx, the plague. The chorus im-
plores Oedipus to save the city.
Oedipus vanquished the Sphinx. He
promises. (*exit*)

After the Prologue, curtain.
On stage: Oedipus, The Chorus

CHORUS

The plague falls on us,
Thebes is dying of plague
From the plague preserve us

qua Theba moritur.
Œdipus, adest pestis;
e peste libera urbem,
urbem serva morientem.

ŒDIPUS

Liberi, vos liberabo a
  peste.
Ego clarissimus Œdipus
  vos diligo,
Eg'Œdipus vos servabo.

CHORUS

Serva nos adhuc.
serva urbem, Œdipus;
serva nos, clarissime Œdipus!
Quid fakiendum, Œdipus,
ut liberemur?

ŒDIPUS

Uxoris frater mittitur
oraculum consulit,
deo mittitur Creo;
oraculum consulit,
quid fakiendum consulit.
Creone commoretur.

Créon paraît

CHORUS

Vale, Creo! Audimus.
Vale, Creo! Kito, kito.
Audituri te salutant.

SPEAKER

Voici Créon, beau-frère d'Œdipe. Il
revient de consulter l'oracle.

L'oracle exige qu'on punisse le
meurtre de Laiüs. L'assassin se cache
dans Thèbes; il faut le découvrir
coûte que coûte.

Œdipe se vante de son adresse à

for Thebes is dying.
Oedipus, the plague has come
free our city from plague
preserve our dying city.

OEDIPUS

Citizens, I shall free you
  from the plague.
I, illustrious Oedipus,
  love you.
I, Oedipus, shall save you.

CHORUS

You can still save us,
preserve our city, Oedipus;
save us, famous Oedipus!
What must be done, Oedipus,
that we may be delivered?

OEDIPUS

The brother of my wife was sent
to consult the oracle,
Creon was sent to the god;
he is asking of the oracle,
he is asking what must be done.
May Creon make haste.

Creon appears

CHORUS

Hail, Creon! We hearken.
Hail, Creon! Speak, speak!
We greet you and hearken.

This is Creon, brother-in-law of
Oedipus. He has returned from consulting the oracle.

The oracle demands that the murder
of Laius be punished. The assassin
is hiding in Thebes; he must be
found at all costs.

Oedipus prides himself on his skill

deviner les énigmes. Il découvrira et
chassera l'assassin. (*exit*)

at solving riddles. He will find
the murderer and drive him out.

CREO

CREON

Respondit deus: -
Laium ulkiski,
skelus ulkiski;
reperire peremptorem.
Thebis peremptor latet.
Latet peremptor regis,
reperire opus istum;
luere Thebas,
Thebas a labe luere,
kaedem regis ulkiski,
regis Laii perempti,
Thebis peremptor latet.
Opus istum reperire,
quem depelli deus jubet.

Peste infikit Thebas. -
Apollo dixit deus.

The god has answered:
Avenge Laius,
avenge the guilt
discover the murderer.
The murderer hides in Thebes,
The murderer of the king hides
and must be discovered;
purge Thebes,
purge Thebes of its stain,
avenge the death of the king,
of the slain King Laius,
the murderer hides in Thebes.
He must be discovered,
for the god demands he be
   driven from us.
He infects Thebes with plague.
Apollo has spoken, the god.

ŒDIPUS

OEDIPUS

Non reperias vetus skelus,
Thebas eruam.
Thebas incolit skelestus.

Since the ancient crime is hidden,
I shall scour Thebes.
The criminal dwells in Thebes.

CHORUS

CHORUS

Deus dixit, tibi dixit.

The god has spoken to you.

ŒDIPUS

OEDIPUS

Tibi dixit.
Miki debet se dedere.
Opus vos istum deferre.
Thebas eruam,
Thebis pellere istum,
Vetus skelus non reperias.

He has spoken to you.
You must have faith in me.
I promise to carry out this task.
I shall scour Thebes,
I shall drive him out of Thebes.
The ancient crime will be avenged.

CHORUS

CHORUS

Thebis skelestus incolit.

The criminal dwells in Thebes.

ŒDIPUS

OEDIPUS

Deus dixit . . .
Sphynga solvi, carmen solvi,

The god has spoken.
I solved the riddle of the Sphinx,

ego divinabo,
Iterum divinabo,
clarissimus Œdipus,
Thebas iterum servabo.
eg'Œdipus carmen divinabo.

I shall divine,
again I shall divine,
I, illustrious Oedipus,
again shall preserve Thebes.
I, Oedipus, shall divine the
    riddle.

CHORUS

CHORUS

Solve! Solve, Œdipus, solve!

Solve it! Solve it, Oedipus,
    Oedipus, solve it!

ŒDIPUS

OEDIPUS

Pollikeor divinabo.
Clarissimus Œdipus,
pollikeor divinabo.

I promise, I shall divine it,
illustrious Oedipus speaks;
I promise, I shall divine it.

SPEAKER

Œdipe interroge la fontaine de
vérité: Tirésias, le devin.

Oedipus questions the fountain of
truth: Tiresias, the seer.

Tirésias évite de répondre. Il n'ignore
plus qu'Œdipe est joué par les
dieux sans coeur.

Tiresias avoids answering. He now
realises that Oedipus is a
plaything of the heartless gods.

Ce silence irrite Œdipe. Il accuse
Créon de vouloir le trône et Tirésias d'être son complice.

This silence angers Oedipus. He
accuses Creon of coveting the
throne and Tiresias of being his
accomplice.

Révolté par cette attitude injuste
Tirésias se décide. La fontaine
parle.

Revolted by this injustice,
Tiresias makes up his mind. The
fountain speaks.

Voici l'oracle: L'assassin du roi
est un roi. (*exit*)

This is the oracle. The murderer of
the king is a king. (*exit*)

CHORUS

CHORUS

Delie, exspectamus.
Minerva, filia Iovis,
Diana in trono insidens,
Et tu, Phaebe
insignis iaculator,
succurrite nobis.
Ut praekeps ales ruit malum
et premitur funere funus
et corporibus corpora inhumata.

God of Delos, we are waiting.
Minerva, daughter of Jove,
Diana enthroned,
and you, Phoebus,
splendid archer,
come to our aid.
For swiftly rushes the winged evil,
death follows hard upon death
and corpses lie unburied in heaps.

82

Expelle, everte in mare
atrokem istum Martem
qui nos urit inermis
dementer ululans.
Et tu, Bakke, cum tæda
advola nobis urens infamem
inter deos deum.

Tirésias paraît

Salve, Tiresia,
homo clare, vates!
Dic nobis quod monet deus,
dic kito, sacrorum docte, dic!

TIRESIAS

Dikere non possum,
dikere non liket,
dikere nefastum;
Œdipus, non possum.
Dikere ne cogas,
cave ne dicam.
Clarissime Œdipus,
takere fas.

ŒDIPUS

Takiturnitas t'acusat:
tu peremptor.

TIRESIAS

Miserande, dico,
quod me acusas, dico.
Dicam quod dixit deus;
nullum dictum kelabo;
inter vos peremptor est,
apud vos peremptor est,
cum vobis, vobiscum est.
Regis est rex peremptor,
Rex kekidit Laium,
rex kekidit regem,
deus regem acusat;
peremptor rex!
Opus Thebis pelli regem.
Rex skelestus urbem fœdat,
rex peremptor regis est.

Drive forth, cast into the sea
the dreadful Mars
who decimates us helpless,
howling madly.
And you Bacchus, come swiftly with
torch to burn out the most infamous
of all the gods.

Tiresias appears

Hail, Tiresias,
famous man, prophet!
Tell us what the god demands,
speak quickly, learned priest, speak!

TIRESIAS

I cannot speak,
I am not allowed to speak,
to speak would be a sin;
Oedipus, I cannot.
Force me not to speak.
I am forbidden to speak.
Illustrious Oedipus,
allow me to be silent.

OEDIPUS

Your silence accuses you;
you are the murderer.

TIRESIAS

Pitiable man, I speak,
since you accuse me, I speak.
I shall speak what the god has said;
no word will I conceal;
the murderer is in your midst,
the murderer is near you,
he is one of you.
The king is the king's murderer.
The king slew Laius,
the king slew the king,
the god accuses your king!
The murderer is a king!
The king must be driven from Thebes.
A guilty king pollutes your city
the king is the king's murderer.

ŒDIPUS

Invidia fortunam odit,
creavistis me regem.
Servavi vos carminibus
et creavistis me regem.
Solvendum carmen,
cui erat solvendum?
Tibi, homo clare, vates;
a me solutum est
et creavistis me regem.
Invidia fortunam odit.
Nunc, vult quidam munus meum,
Creo vult munus regis.
Stipendarius est, Tiresia!
Hoc fakinus ego solvo!
Creo vult rex fieri,
Quis liberavit vos carminibus?
Amiki! Eg' Œdipus clarus, ego.
Invidia fortunam odit.
Volunt regem perire,
vestrum regem perire,
clarum Œdipodem, vestrum regem.

Jocaste paraît

CHORUS

Gloria!
Laudibus regina Jocasta
in pestilentibus Thebis.
Laudibus regina nostra.
Laudibus Œdipodis uxor.
Gloria!

ACT II

Rideau, En scène: Œdipe, Jocaste,
Le Chœur.
Reprise du dernier Chœur
Entrée du Speaker

SPEAKER

La dispute des princes attire
Jocaste.
Vous allez l'entendre les calmer,
leur faire honte de vociférer

OEDIPUS

Envy hates the fortunate.
You made me king.
I saved you by answering the riddles
and you made me king.
The riddle had to be solved,
who was to solve it?
You, famous man, prophet?
It was solved by me,
and you made me king.
Envy hates the fortunate.
Now there is one who wants my place,
Creon wants the king's place.
You have been bribed, Tiresias!
I shall lay bare this plot!
Creon would be king.
Who freed you from the riddles?
Friends, it was I, famed Oedipus, I.
Envy hates the fortunate.
They want to destroy the king,
to destroy your king,
famed Oedipus, your king.

Jocasta appears

CHORUS

Glory!
All praise to queen Jocasta
in plague-ridden Thebes.
All praise to our queen.
All praise to Oedipus' wife
Glory!

Curtain, On stage: Oedipus, Jocasta,
The Chorus.
Repeat of the last Chorus
Entry of the Speaker

The dispute of the princes attracts
Jocasta.
You will hear her calm
them, shame them for raising their

dans une ville malade.

Elle ne croit pas aux oracles. Elle prouve que les oracles mentent. Par exemple on avait prédit que Laiüs mourrait par un fils d'elle; or Laiüs a été assassiné par des voleurs au carrefour des trois routes de Daulie et de Delphes.

Trivium! Carrefour! Retenez bien ce mot. Il épouvante Œdipe. Il se souvient qu'arrivant de Corinthe, avant sa rencontre avec le sphinx, il a tué un vieillard au carrefour des trois routes. Si c'est Laiüs, que devenir? Car il ne peut retourner à Corinthe, l'oracle l'ayant menacé de tuer son père et d'épouser sa mère. Il a peur. (*exit*)

JOCASTA

Nonn'erubeskite, reges,
clamare, ululare in ægra urbe
domestikis altercationibus?
Nonn'erubeskite in ægra urbe
clamare vestros domestikos clamores?
Coram omnibus clamare,
coram omnibus domestikos clamores,
clamare in ægra urbe, reges,
nonn'erubeskite?
Ne probentur oracula
quæ semper mentiantur.
Oracula – mentita sunt oracula.
Cui rex interfikiendus est?
Nato meo.
Age rex peremptus est.
Laius in trivio mortuus.
Ne probentur oracula
quæ semper mentiantur.
Cave oracula.

CHORUS

Trivium, trivium . . .

voices in a stricken city.

She does not believe in oracles. She proves that oracles lie. For example, it was foretold that Laius would die at the hands of a son of hers; but Laius was murdered by thieves, at the junction of the three roads from Daulis and Delphi.

Trivium! Junction! Remember that word. It terrifies Oedipus. He remembers how, arriving from Corinth before his encounter with the Sphinx, he killed an old man at the junction of three roads. If that was Laius, what then? For he cannot return to Corinth, the oracle having threatened him with killing his father and marrying his mother. He is afraid. (*exit*)

JOCASTA

Are you not ashamed, princes,
to bicker and howl in a stricken city,
raising up your personal broils?
Are you not ashamed in a stricken city
to complain your personal complaints?
To clamour before everyone,
before everyone to raise up
your personal broils in a stricken city,
are you not ashamed, princes?
Oracles are not to be trusted,
they always lie.
Oracles – they are all liars.
By whom was the king to be slain?
By my son.
Well, the king was slain.
Laius died at the crossroads.
Oracles are not to be trusted,
they always lie.
Beware of oracles.

CHORUS

The crossroads, the crossroads . . .

ŒDIPUS

Pavesco subito, Jocasta,
pavesco maxime. Jocasta audi:
locuta es de trivio?
Ego senem kekidi,
cum Corintho exkederem,
kekidi in trivio,
kekidi, Jocasta, senem.

OEDIPUS

I am afraid suddenly, Jocasta,
I have great fear, Jocasta, listen:
did you speak of the crossroads?
I killed an old man
when I was coming from Corinth,
killed him at the crossroads,
I killed, Jocasta, an old man.

JOCASTA

Oracula mentiuntur,
semper oracula mentiuntur,
Œdipus, cave oracula;
quæ mentiantur.
Domum kito redeamus.
Non est consulendum.

JOCASTA

Oracles are liars,
oracles are always liars,
Oedipus, beware of oracles;
they tell lies.
Let us return home quickly,
there is no truth here.

ŒDIPUS

Pavesco, maxime pavesco,
pavesco subito, Jocasta;
pavor magnus, Jocasta,
in me inest.
Subito pavesco, uxor Jocasta.
Nam in trivio kekidi senem.

Volo consulere,
consulendum est, Jocasta,
volo videre pastorem.
Skeleris superest spectator

Jocasta, consulendum,
volo consulere. Skiam!

OEDIPUS

I am afraid, greatly afraid,
I am afraid suddenly, Jocasta;
a great fear, Jocasta,
has come upon me.
Suddenly I fear, Jocasta, my wife.
For I killed an old man at the cross-
    roads.
I want to find out the truth,
there is truth, Jocasta,
I want to see the shepherd.
He still lives, he who witnessed the
    crime.
Jocasta, the truth,
I must find out the truth. I must know!

SPEAKER

Le témoin du meurtre sort de l'ombre.
Un messager annonce à Œdipe la mort
de Polybe et lui révèle qu'il n'était
que son fils adoptif.

The witness of the murder emerges
from the shadow. A messenger announces to Oedipus that Polybus is
dead and that he was only his
adopted son.

Jocaste comprend.

Jocasta understands.

Elle tente de tirer Œdipe en
arrière. Elle se sauve.

She tries to draw Oedipus back. She
flees.

Œdipe la croit honteuse d'être une femme de parvenu.

Oedipus thinks she is ashamed to be the wife of an upstart.

Cet Œdipe, si fier de deviner tout! Il est dans le piège. Il est le seul à ne pas s'en apercevoir.

This Oedipus, so proud of understanding everything! He is in the trap. He is the only one who does not see it.

La vérité le frappe sur la tête.

The truth strikes him on the head.

Il tombe. Il tombe de haut. (*exit*)

He falls. He falls headlong. (*exit*)

Entrée du Berger et du Messager

Enter the Shepherd and the Messenger

CHORUS

CHORUS

Adest omniskius pastor
et nuntius horribilis.

The shepherd who knows all is here,
and the messenger of dread tidings.

NUNTIO

MESSENGER

Mortuus est Polybus.
Senex mortuus Polybus
non genitor Œdipodis;
a me keperat Polybus,
eg' attuleram regi.

Polybus is dead.
Old Polybus is dead;
he was not Oedipus' father;
Polybus got him from me;
I took him to the king.

CHORUS

CHORUS

Verus non fuerat pater Œdipodis.

He was not Oedipus' real father.

NUNTIO

MESSENGER

Falsus pater per me!

His feigned father, by my doing!

CHORUS

CHORUS

Falsus pater per te!

His feigned father, by your doing!

NUNTIO

MESSENGER

Reppereram in monte
puerum Œdipoda,
derelictum in monte
parvulum Œdipoda
foratum pedes,
vulneratum pedes,
parvulum Œdipoda.
Reppereram in monte,
attuleram pastori
puerum Œdipoda.

I found on the mountain
the child Oedipus,
abandoned on the mountain,
the infant Oedipus,
his feet pierced,
his feet wounded,
the infant Oedipus.
I found on the mountain
and took to the shepherd
the child Oedipus.

87

CHORUS

Reskiturus sum monstrum,
monstrum reskiskam.
Deo claro Œdipus natus est,
deo et nympha montium
in quibus repertus est.

PASTOR

Oportebat takere, nunquam loqui.
Sane repperit parvulum Œdipoda.
A patre, a matre
in monte derelictum
pedes laqueis foratum.
Utinam ne dikeres;
hoc semper kelandum
inventum esse in monte
derelictum parvulum,
parvum Œdipoda,
in monte derelictum.
Oportebat takere, nunquam loqui.

Jocaste disparaît

ŒDIPUS

Nonne monstrum reskituri
quis Œdipus, genus Œdipodis skiam.
Pudet Jocastam, fugit.
Pudet Œdipi exulis,
pudet Œdipodis generis.
Skiam Œdipodis genus;
genus meum skiam.
Nonne monstrum reskituri
genus Œdipodis skiam,
genus exulis mei.
Ego exul exsulto.

PASTOR ET NUNTIO

In monte reppertus est,
a matre derelictus;
a matre derelictum
in montibus repperimus.
Laio Jocastaque natus!
Peremptor Laii parentis!
Coniux Jocastæ parentis!
Utinam ne dikeres,

CHORUS

I am about to hear a marvel.
I shall hear a marvel.
Oedipus was born of a great god,
of a god and a nymph of the mountain
on which he was found.

SHEPHERD

Silence were better, not speech.
Indeed he found the infant Oedipus,
by father, by mother
abandoned on the mountain,
his feet pierced with thongs.
You should not have spoken:
this should always have been hidden,
that the abandoned infant
was found on the mountain,
the infant Oedipus,
abandoned on the mountain.
Silence were better, not speech.

Exit Jocasta

OEDIPUS

If the marvel be not revealed,
I shall find out Oedipus' lineage.
Jocasta is ashamed, she flees.
She is ashamed of Oedipus the exile,
she is ashamed of Oedipus' parents.
I shall find out Oedipus' lineage;
I shall find out my origin.
If the marvel be not revealed,
I shall find out Oedipus' lineage,
the origin of my exile.
I, an exile, exult.

SHEPHERD AND MESSENGER

On the mountain he was found,
abandoned by his mother;
by his mother abandoned,
we found him on the mountain.
He is the son of Laius and Jocasta,
the slayer of Laius, his parent,
the husband of Jocasta, his parent!
You should not have spoken,

opportebat takere,
nunquam dikere istud:
a Jocasta derelictus
in monte reppertus est.

Le Berger et le Messager s'éloignent

ŒDIPUS

Natus sum quo nefastum est,
concubui cui nefastum est,
kekidi quem nefastum est.
Lux facta est! (*exit*)

Le Messager apparaît

SPEAKER

Et maintenant, vous allez entendre
le monologue illustre 'LA TÊTE DIV-
INE DE JOCASTE EST MORTE',
monologue où le messager raconte la fin
de Jocaste.

Il peut à peine ouvrir la bouche. Le
chœur emprunte son rôle et l'aide à
dire comment la reine s'est pendue et
comment Œdipe s'est crevé les yeux
avec son agrafe d'or.

Ensuite c'est l'épilogue.

Epilogue. Le roi est pris. Il veut
se montrer à tous, montrer la bête
immonde, l'inceste, le parricide, le
fou.

On le chasse. On le chasse avec une
extrême douceur. Adieu, adieu, pauvre
Œdipe! Adieu, Œdipe; on t'aimait.

NUNTIO

Divum Jocastæ caput mortuum!

CHORUS

Mulier in vestibulo
comas lakerare.
Claustris occludere fores,
occludere, exclamare.

---

silence would have been best,
never to speak this thing:
abandoned by Jocasta,
he was found on the mountain.

Exeunt the Shepherd and the Messenger

OEDIPUS

I was born of whom divine law forbade,
I have lain with whom divine law forbade,
I have slain whom divine law forbade.
All now is made clear! (*exit*)

The Messenger appears

SPEAKER

And now you will hear the famous
monologue 'THE DIVINE JOCASTA IS
DEAD', a monologue in which the
messenger describes the death of
Jocasta.

He can scarcely open his mouth.
The chorus takes his part and helps
him tell how the queen has hanged
herself and how Oedipus has gouged
out his eyes with her golden clasp.

Then comes the epilogue.

Epilogue. The king is caught. He
wishes to show himself to all,
show the foul beast, the incestuous
parricide, the madman.

They drive him away. Drive him away
with extreme gentleness. Farewell,
farewell, poor Oedipus! Farewell,
Oedipus; you were loved.

MESSENGER

The divine Jocasta is dead!

CHORUS

The woman in the courtyard
tore at her hair.
She made fast the doors,
shut in and crying aloud.

Et Œdipus irrumpere,
irrumpere et pulsare,
et Œdipus pulsare, ululare.

NUNTIO

Divum Jocastæ caput mortuum!

CHORUS

Et ubi evellit claustra,
suspensam mulierem
omnes conspexerunt.
Et Œdipus prækeps ruens
illam exsolvebat, illam collocabat;
illam exsolvere, illam collocare.
Et aurea fibula et avulsa fibula

oculos effodire;
ater sanguis rigare.

NUNTIO

Divum Jocastæ caput mortuum!

CHORUS

Sanguis ater rigabat;
ater sanguis prosiliebat;
et Œdipus exclamare
et sese detestare.
Omnibus se ostendere.
Aspikite fores pandere,
spectaculum aspikite,
spectaculum omnium atrokissimum.

NUNTIO

Divum Jocastæ caput mortuum!

Œdipe réapparaît

Le Messager disparaît

CHORUS

Ekke! Regem Œdipoda,
fœdissimum monstrum monstrat
fœdissimam beluam.
Ellum, regem Œdipoda!
Ellum, regem okkekatum!

And Oedipus burst in,
burst in and pounded on the doors,
and Oedipus pounded, howling wildly.

MESSENGER

The divine Jocasta is dead!

CHORUS

And when they broke open the lock,
everyone beheld
the woman hanging.
And Oedipus, rushing headlong,
loosened her and laid her down;
loosened her, laid her down,
and with a golden brooch plucked
  from her
he gouged out his eyes;
the black blood flowed.

MESSENGER

The divine Jocasta is dead!

CHORUS

The black blood flowed,
the black blood gushed forth;
and Oedipus cried aloud
and cursed himself.
He shows himself to all.
Behold through the open doors,
behold the sad spectacle,
the most horrible of all sights.

MESSENGER

The divine Jocasta is dead!

Oedipus reappears

Exit the Messenger

CHORUS

Behold! Oedipus the king,
appears a most foul monster,
a most foul beast.
Lo, Oedipus the king!
Lo, the blind king!

Rex parrikida, miser Œdipus,
miser rex Œdipus carminum coniector
Adest! Ellum! Regem Œdipoda!
Vale, Œdipus,
te amabam, te miseror.
Miser Œdipus, oculos tuos deploro.

Vale, Œdipus,
miser Œdipus noster,
te amabam, Œdipus.
Tibi valedico, Œdipus,
tibi valedico.

Rideau

The parricide king, poor Oedipus,
poor King Oedipus, solver of riddles.
He is here! Lo! Oedipus the king!
Farewell, Oedipus,
I loved you, I pity you.
Wretched Oedipus, I lament the loss of
  your eyes.

Farewell, Oedipus,
our poor Oedipus,
I loved you, Oedipus,
I bid you farewell, Oedipus
I bid you farewell.

Curtain

(English translation from the Latin by
e. e. cummings; from the French by
Stephen Walsh)

Appendix B

The Latin text and its setting

The evolution of the final Latin text of *Oedipus rex* is hard if not impossible to reconstruct. Cocteau completed his first draft in late October 1925, but this seems to have been the text he later published as an independent play called *Oedipe-Roi*, which coincides only in isolated passages with the eventual Latin. On the other hand, published French versions of Daniélou's text digress from the play even in many of the coincident passages, encouraging the speculation that they are indeed translations from the Latin rather than printings of Cocteau's French text as sent to Daniélou, which seems not to have survived. It would be useful to have the original French, if only to check the exact form of the text as it reached the translator, as this would presumably then reveal, beyond serious doubt, the form of Daniélou's text as it reached Stravinsky. This in turn would tell us to what extent the complicated scheme of line and phrase repetitions so characteristic of the score was Stravinsky's work, and to what extent it originated with the librettist or translator. Daniélou's text is not at all a routine Latinisation, but a skilful classical conceit in which assonance, interior rhyme, pleonasm, chiasmus, and other devices work so well towards the composer's musical intentions that it is hard to believe that there was no direct collaboration between them, as all the incidental documentation seems to suggest.

An example will help clarify the point. In the play, Jocasta's first speech runs: 'Princes, ne rougissez-vous pas de cette scène de famille dans une ville qui souffre? Ne rougissez-vous pas de vociférer dans une ville malade?' ('Princes, do you not blush at this family row in a stricken city? Do you not blush to raise your voices in a sick city?'). The full Latin equivalent to this is:

> Nonn'erubeskite, reges, (*repeated*)
> clamare, ululare in ægra urbe
> domestikis altercationibus,
> reges, nonn'erubeskite?
> Nonn'erubeskite in ægra urbe

92

clamare vestros domestikos clamores
in ægra urbe?
Nonn'erubeskite altercationibus, reges? etc.

No doubt every specific Latin phrase came from Daniélou. But were the repetitions and reorderings his, or did they come from Cocteau in his second draft, and/or did they arise from Stravinsky's express musical needs? The structure is so literate, as well as cunning, that it seems likely to be Daniélou's. Moreover, a glance at the libretto (Appendix A) shows that such procedures are normal throughout *Oedipus rex*. I drew attention in chapter 3 to the obsessive character of the repetitions in Oedipus's 'Invidia fortunam odit', and the way the music echoes them. Stravinsky may well have had at the back of his mind the *ad hoc* repetitions whereby the exiguous texts of baroque operatic arias are made to serve elaborate musical forms. But a subtler explanation of these jugglings with words and phrases is to be found in his own style and musical thought, whose roots go deep into his Russian past. That the form of the text answered his specific requirements can hardly be doubted. But how they were transmitted remains to some extent a mystery.

In a fascinating paper based on a study of the ethnic sources of works such as the *Pribaoutki*, the *Podbliudnye* ('Saucers') choruses and *Les Noce*s, Richard Taruskin has traced the origins of Stravinsky's love of accentual and metric paradox to Russian folk collections and ethnographic studies that were known to him when he was writing or sketching those works (1914–15).[1] Stravinsky was, however, predisposed to metric experiment, as the *Three Japanese Lyrics* show (to say nothing of instrumental works like the last of the piano studies, op. 7, or indeed *Petrushka* and *The Rite of Spring*). What his 'rejoicing discovery' provided was a living verbal model which mapped perfectly on to his musical and poetic obsessions of the time. It also in due course helped him evolve a highly adaptable metric technique which could be extended into purely instrumental works, or later into settings of other languages. Taruskin was not the first to point out that Stravinsky's supposed misaccentuations of French (in *Persephone*) and English (in *The Rake's Progress* and elsewhere) were a deliberate application of the 'rejoicing discovery' to languages to which, in terms of strict idiom, it was inappropriate.

The case of *Oedipus rex*, however, is slightly different, since, although the accentuation of spoken and poetic Latin is known, the language is now sufficiently distanced from usage and common experience for distortions to take on a purely contextual significance. That is, the listener might accept Oēdǐpǔs or Oědīpǔs, but if he hears both in sequence he suspects a manipulation. No doubt this was precisely one of the attractions of the language for Stravinsky. In setting Russian, especially folk verse, he could tinker with the accents knowing that the style was authentic and that, still more important, he would understand as well as anybody just what the effect on a Russophone listener would be. French and English offered no such guarantees. But in Latin the second consideration was irrelevant, while the first was thus rendered practically unimportant.[2]

In his Russian settings, Stravinsky not only often works the musical accent against the verbal, but he also juxtaposes different accentuations or metric placings of a given word, and he favours texts rich in verbal plays, varied repetitions, alliterations, and other devices that tend to draw attention away from the word as meaning (semanteme) and towards the word as sound (phoneme). His treatment of Daniélou's Latin is somewhat in the same spirit, especially where particular words, like 'oracula' and 'trivium', are harped on. For instance, in the reprise of the slow section of Jocasta's aria the single sentence 'Ne probentur oracula, quae semper mentiantur' is laid on to the existing music (originally set to the much longer text quoted above) with studied disregard for any possible single metric pattern or any systematic scheme of repetition, but in such a way as to bring together conflicting accentuations of 'oracula'. The effect is curious. No longer is there any sense of rustic pleasure at kicking words round the football pitch of language; but instead Jocasta, with her conventionalised (da capo) music, her seemingly arbitrary twisting and turning back on to the same verbal ideas, and her mantric experiments with particular words, is more than ever stripped of mind and volition and abandoned like a straw to the winds of fate. Thus also the chorus's play with the accentuation of 'Oedipus' or the Messenger's with that of 'Polybus'. Not only is the speaker implicitly rendered helpless, but also perhaps the person referred to. If the pronunciation of his name is in doubt, so surely is his identity. The ambiguous accent is like yet another mask, concealing the individual and limiting his self-determination, or even (in the case of the adoptive father Polybus) casting doubt on his very existence.

No doubt too much should not be made of such hidden meanings. Stravinsky came to Latin first and foremost as a 'free' language which could be treated unconcernedly as verbal music. Among other things, the accentual plays serve to offset music which, by Stravinsky's standards, is unusually periodic and metrically regular. They work against a background of plain repetition and metronomically even note values which still hark back in many respects to the 'monometric' works of a decade or so earlier. But the accentual equivocations in *Oedipus* are less playful, more ponderous, than those in the Russian works, and mark a new phase in his treatment of language – a phase that would lead soon to the Latin settings in the *Symphony of Psalms* (which Taruskin believes to have been composed initially to the Russian words), the French settings of *Persephone*, to which its author, André Gide, took such exception, and the English of *The Rake's Progress*, which so brilliantly matches the artifice of the Auden/Kallman text.

Appendix C

Cast and orchestra

Oedipus	tenor
Jocasta	mezzo-soprano
Creon	bass-baritone
Tiresias	bass
Shepherd	tenor
Messenger	bass-baritone
Chorus	tenors/basses

3 flutes (3rd doubles piccolo)	4 horns (F)
2 oboes	4 trumpets (C)
cor anglais	3 trombones
3 clarinets (B♭ & A) (3rd doubles E♭)	tuba
2 bassoons	timpani
double bassoon	percussion (side drum, tambourine, cymbals, bass drum)
	harp
	piano
strings	

Oedipus was Stravinsky's first entirely new work for anything like a 'standard' orchestra since *Pulcinella* (1919), and his first for a full symphony orchestra since *The Rite of Spring* (1913). The orchestra itself, with its triple woodwind and four trumpets, is a fairly normal high-romantic one (*cf.* Wagner's *Tristan und Isolde* or Tchaikovsky's *Manfred* Symphony), but appreciably smaller than in Stravinsky's own early ballets, where quadruple woodwind is a working minimum and the percussion sections are much bigger (*The Rite of Spring* has quintuple woodwind and a double-sized brass section). The single un-Tchaikovskian feature of the *Oedipus* orchestra is the E♭ clarinet. *Manfred* does not have a piano. But that instrument had already become a fairly normal extra in Russian theatre scores, ever since its use by Glinka in *Ruslan and Lyudmila*.

But while the orchestra may be conventional, its treatment certainly is not. The scoring still reflects the recent predominance of wind instruments and piano in Stravinsky's music. The upper strings, especially, are very lightly used indeed, and rarely assert their traditional role as bedrock orchestral sonority. For long stretches they are completely silent. In the first scene, for instance, the first violins have more than eighty bars' rest before the entry of Creon and are then largely silent through the first part of his aria. One of the reasons for the rather splashy effect of their *fortissimo* entry at fig. 40 (Stravinsky's 'the girls enter kicking'[1]) is that this is the first time in the work that violins and violas have been heard in a significant melody. Later, the strings are most likely to resume their traditional role in quiet music: for instance, at Oedipus's more inward moments, such as 'Invidia fortunam odit', or when Jocasta calms the disputing princes. But even here Stravinsky never lets the string sound become a routine support, and upper strings are surprisingly silent throughout the slow section of Jocasta's 'Nonn'erubeskite', where one might have supposed that the Verdian reference would have demanded their use.

Woodwind and/or brass often simply replace the strings in this supporting role, continuing the manner of the Concerto for piano and wind: for instance the wind accompaniment of 'E peste serva nos' (fig. 6), with horns supplying the harmonic and rhythmic stuffing that might more conventionally come from the lower strings. Often this preoccupation with the wind takes on a certain ostentatious conventionality: textures will be reinforced or mobilised by arpeggios for trombones (around fig. 39 in Creon's aria), or clarinets (Jocasta's 'Ne probentur oracula', fig. 100), or bassoons (Oedipus's 'Nonne monstrum', fig. 152). But the wind scoring also has an emblematic force not so noticeable in the string writing. At solemn moments it is the wind choir that speaks: at Tiresias's 'Miserande, dico', where the radiance of the sudden A minor chord announces as clearly as words that what the seer is about to say will be divinely inspired; or at the chorus's 'Reskiturus sum monstrum' (fig. 144), which hints at the intervention of the gods in Oedipus's birth; or even in the *ranz des vaches* bassoon duet which accompanies the Shepherd, since his pastoral calling is itself semi-divine and implies 'insight'.

These tendencies are still essentially those of the early twenties, when Stravinsky had written that wind instruments seemed 'more apt to tender a certain rigidity of the form I had in mind than other instruments'.[2] What is new (for him) in this treatment is the symbolic force of the quasi-archaic, quasi-primitive wind sound. Wind instruments had traditionally accompanied public ceremonies (as they still do) because of their carrying power, and much of Stravinsky's brass writing – especially of course the trumpet fanfares and flourishes – alludes to this idea in a strictly orthodox sense. But the idea of wind instruments as, perhaps literally, divinely inspired comes from baroque opera, via certain nineteenth-century composers such as Berlioz (whose *L'Enfance du Christ* often comes to mind as one listens to Stravinsky) and Tchaikovsky, whose astonishing ear for woodwind sound must surely have impressed his younger compatriot. One needs look no farther than the coda of *Romeo and Juliet* for a brilliant expression of the idea of numinous wind-scoring as a beatification in times of disaster.

The percussion scoring in *Oedipus* is restrained for the composer of *The Rite of Spring* and *Les Noces*, and its most telling effects are quiet and menacing, rather than violent. The soft timpani accompaniment to Oedipus's confessional 'Ego senem kekidi' (fig. 119) has a dramatic force in inverse proportion to its volume, and the timpani rolls that sometimes accompany the Speaker are similarly like the distant rumble of divine thunder. These sounds must surely have been in Britten's ears when he set the passage from Wordsworth's *Prelude* in his *Nocturne*. The timpani also contribute decisively to Oedipus's culminating 'Lux facta est'; but again the contribution is restrained, almost to the point of inaudibility. The other main percussion instrument is the piano – also an instrument Stravinsky favoured in the early twenties because of its capacity for hard, incisive articulation and its inherent resistance to a smooth, unbreathing legato. The piano gives bite to the ostinato writing in *Oedipus*. But it is never an obbligato instrument in the *Petrushka* sense. Its general function is to delineate rhythm in choruses or orchestral tutti, where the pulse might otherwise tend to become blurred. Stravinsky greatly extended this idea in the *Symphony of Psalms* three years later, and still further in the *Symphony in three movements*, where the piano writing has once more grown to the status of an obbligato solo.

Notes

1 The exile finds a new home

1 Stravinsky's letter is in *Le Figaro*, 18 May 1922; reprinted in Lesure, *Stravinsky: Études et témoignages*, and quoted in English in *SPD*, pp. 231–2.

2 Later came: Stravinsky, 'Some ideas about my Octuor'; A. Lourié, 'La Sonate pour piano de Strawinsky'; Lourié, 'Oedipus Rex'; Lourié, 'A propos de l'*Apollon* d'Igor Strawinsky'.

3 There is an echo of this attitude in Aldous Huxley's *Antic Hay* (1923), where Gumbril anathematises Scriabin as '*le Tschaikovsky de nos jours*'.

4 *Le Coq et l'arlequin* (1918), in Cocteau, *Le Rappel à l'ordre*, p. 29.

5 Ibid, p. 17.

6 *Les Nouvelles Littéraires*, 8 December 1928, quoted in *SPD*, p. 164.

7 See the preface to the published score.

8 *Art et scolastique* (L'Art Catholique: Paris, 1920).

9 He himself denied any such influence. See *Expo*, p. 76.

10 Ibid.

11 See his letter of 6 April to Diaghilev, asking for his forgiveness 'before the Confession'. *SSCII*, pp. 40–1. The Podossenov letters, in closely written Russian, are in the Paul Sacher Stiftung in Basel.

12 *SPD*, p. 211.

13 *Dial*, p. 26. This is a convenient place to correct an error in my book *The Music of Stravinsky*, p. 306, n. 2, concerning the first performance of the Sonata. I was right in saying that Stravinsky did not himself play the Sonata at Donaueschingen in July 1925. It was however played there none the less, on 16 July, by Felix Petyrek, as an entry in Werner Zintgraf's *Neue Musik: Donaueschingen 1921–1950* (Geiger-Verlag: Horb am Neckar, nd), p. 28, proves. I am grateful to Horst Koegler for bringing this to my attention.

14 *Dial*, p. 21.

15 Joergensen (trans. Wyzewa), *Saint François d'Assise: sa vie et son oeuvre*, p. 43. Reference is to the 1935 edition, but the translation was first published in 1910.

16 Daniélou (1905–74) was a twenty-year-old student at the Sorbonne when he translated *Oedipus*, having probably, according to Cocteau's biographer, Francis Steegmuller, been recommended to Cocteau by Maritain. See *Cocteau: a Biography*, p. 358. Daniélou's subsequent career was distinguished. He became a Jesuit priest, professor of theology, cardinal (in 1969), and finally French Academician and

Chevalier of the Légion d'Honneur. He played a prominent 'steadying' role in the *Aggiornamento* which led in 1962 to the Second Vatican Council. He was also a prolific writer on theology and the liturgy, but the *Oedipus* translation seems to have been his only professional contact with the arts, and after 1926 he faded out of both Stravinsky's and Cocteau's lives. See *Dial*, p. 30 and Daniélou's obituary in *The Times* (London), 22 May 1974.

17 He never again set a Russian text after *Mavra*. The texts of the original versions of his *Lord's Prayer* (1926), *Creed* (1932) and *Hail Mary* (1934) are in church Slavonic. Musically these works are of little importance, but it cannot be wholly insignificant that the first of them was written at the time of *Oedipus rex*, his first Latin work.

18 The letter, dated 11 October, is given in French in *Dial*, p. 135, and in English in *SSCI*, pp. 94–5.

19 Stravinsky did not meet Maritain until June 1926, two months after his formal return to the church. However Robert Craft, in his diary, suggests that Maritain was partly responsible for the composer's reconversion. See *Stravinsky: The Chronicle of a Friendship 1948–1971*, p. 8.

20 But in the first performance of Stravinsky's *Soldier's Tale*, at Lausanne in 1918, the Narrator had also worn a dinner jacket. The first productions of both Cocteau adaptations were designed by Gabrielle ('Coco') Chanel, a former mistress of Stravinsky and soon to be an important player in the intricate negotiations leading up to the first performance of *Oedipus rex*.

21 *SSCI*, p. 94, n. 38; *Dial*, pp. 22–3. The first draft is apparently the same as the play *Oedipe-Roi* which Cocteau told Stravinsky had been commissioned coincidentally by the Comédie Française in April 1926. The published text bears the same end date 27 October 1925, only sixteen days after the composer's initial 'business' letter. See also Cocteau's letter of 1 May 1926 in *SSCI*, p. 100.

22 See *SSCI*, p. 95, n. 39, and *SPD*, p. 264. Craft (*SSCI*, p. 94, n. 38) follows Francis Steegmuller (*Cocteau*, p. 355) in asserting that the first Cocteau draft was sent to Jean Daniélou for translation into Latin. But Steegmuller gives no source for this information. Stravinsky's own autobiography gives only the bald fact that 'at the opening of the New Year I received from Cocteau the first part of his final version of *Oedipus* in the Latin translation of Jean Daniélou' (*Chron*, p. 209). But this is an unreliable source, even for events that were recent at the time (1935).

23 See for instance Cocteau's letter of 6 March 1926 in *SSCI*, p. 96. But the translation there is faulty: 'Il commence à voir le détail sans perdre de vue notre bloc' – 'He is starting to see the detail without losing sight of our block [design]' (rather than 'I am starting to work . . .').

24 C. Tappolet (ed.), *Correspondance Ansermet–Strawinsky* (1914–67), vol. 2, p. 127. English text in *SSCI*, p. 186.

25 The main sources for these datings are the sketches in the Paul Sacher Stiftung, Basel; the draft piano-vocal score in the Library of Congress, Washington; *SPD*, pp. 264–7; and Vera Stravinsky's diaries as published in R. Craft (ed.), *Dearest Bubushkin*.

26 Letter of 10 February: *SSCI*, p. 102; French original in *Dial*, p. 138.

27 *SSCI*, p. 101. But the English text is garbled from line 2. The original reads: '2. Téléphone de Vera perdu – envoie-le – impossible de lui faire signe pour le jour de l'an. 3. La Princesse est venue me voir. Elle est heureuse de notre collaboration. Elle montre . . .' etc. ('2. I've lost Vera's telephone number – send it – impossible to let her know about New Year's Day. 3. The Princess came to see me. She is happy about our collaboration. She shows . . .' etc.).

28 *SSCI*, p. 103.

29 According to Cocteau, however, Chanel denied a 'dérobade' (deliberate evasion). This is the word marked '[illegible]' in *SSCI*, p. 110 (letter of 24 April 1927).

30 See his letter to Stravinsky of about 22 April 1927, in *SSCI*, 109–10. 'I do not reproach her for it: *mondain* people are all the same.'

31 Ibid, p. 110.

32 See Stravinsky's telegram of late March 1927 in *SSCI*, p. 104, and his letter of 11 April 1927, ibid, pp. 108–9 (French original of the letter in *Dial*, pp. 140–1). But it is the telegram which needs to be checked against the (unpublished) original French: 'Suis reconnaissant Chanel pas prêter attention potins' ('I am grateful to [not 'wary of'] Chanel pay no attention to gossip').

33 According to Otto Klemperer, who was present, the accompaniment was played four-hands by Stravinsky and Prokofiev. See Heyworth, *Conversations with Klemperer*, p. 60. In his biography of Klemperer, Heyworth repeats this story, with the additional remark that the accompaniment was played on two pianos. See *Otto Klemperer: his Life and Times*, vol. 1, p. 246. But there is no four-hand version of *Oedipus rex*, and Vittorio Rieti, who was also present, told me that he had no recollection of Prokofiev's being there at all. Prokofiev's new ballet, *Le Pas d'acier*, also had its première in the Ballets Russes spring season of 1927.

34 *Dial*, pp. 24–5.

2 Of masks, masses and magic

1 *Dial*, p. 30.

2 *Dial*, p. 29.

3 See E. Braun (ed.), *Meyerhold on Theatre*, pp. 70–1, and Braun, *The Director and the Stage*, pp. 120–4.

4 Translated as 'The fairground booth' in *Meyerhold on Theatre*, pp. 119–43.

5 Ibid, p. 127. Similar ideas had been expressed in print in Russia before. See, for instance, the poet Valery Bryussov's attack on the realist theatre in an article called 'The unnecessary truth' in *Mir Isskustva* (1902), together with the editorial comment (possibly by Diaghilev): 'Until the old, conventional, realistic theatre disappears . . . no development in drama can be expected', quoted in R. Buckle, *Diaghilev*, pp. 74–5.

6 In *Expo* (p. 91) Stravinsky says that the Narrator device in *The Soldier's Tale* came from Pirandello (via Pitoëff, according to White, *Stravinsky: the Composer and his*

Works, p. 265). But it seems unlikely that either Stravinsky or Pitoëff (or indeed Ramuz) can have encountered the earliest relevant Pirandello play, *Così è (se vi pare)* (1917), by 1918, the year of *The Soldier's Tale*.

7 'The fairground booth', *Meyerhold on Theatre*, p. 128. See chap. 4 for an account of a production of *Oedipus rex* with puppets.

8 'The stylized theatre', *Meyerhold on Theatre*, pp. 63–4.

9 'The new theatre foreshadowed in literature', *Meyerhold on Theatre*, p. 36. Meyerhold in fact cites Sophocles's *Oedipus at Colonus*, rather than *Oedipus Tyrannus*, as an example of static tragedy. But from Stravinsky's point of view it is not an important distinction.

10 *Dial*, p. 24.

11 Stravinsky was in Paris for a concert performance of *Mavra* on 26 December 1922, then again from 9 January. But in *Chron* (p. 205) he reports having 'just seen' *Antigone* at the time of his return to Nice from Italy in late September 1925.

12 Letter of 11 October; see chap. 1, n. 18.

13 *Dial*, p. 22.

14 Letter of 19 January; *SSCI*, p. 95, n. 19. Assuming that the published *Oedipe-Roi* is more or less the first draft text, it contains internal evidence that no narrator was yet intended. Several phrases eventually allocated to the Speaker occur verbatim in the body of the text: for instance, 'L'assassin se cache dans Thèbes', the crucial 'L'assassin du roi est un roi', and 'La tête divine de Jocaste est morte', which – although the Speaker tells us we are about to hear the monologue whose first line it is – clearly only came his way at all because the monologue had been cut. Oedipus's 'je n'ose revenir à Corinthe où me ménacent le parricide et l'inceste', in the draft, merely clarifies a point that is understood in any case, whereas its equivalent in the opera-oratorio, in the narration at the start of Act II, further obscures the unexplained by the omission of the crucial word 'où' ('where').

15 *Expo*, p. 91: 'I was attracted by this idea, but then I am always attracted by new conditions, and those of the theatre are, to me, a great part of its appeal.'

16 *Dial*, p. 30.

17 'The fairground booth', *Meyerhold on Theatre*, p. 141. His italics.

18 *SSCI*, p. 95. The 'masses' (same word in the French original) are presumably the monumental units of the décor, referred to a few weeks later by Cocteau in his notes for the *Oedipus* sets, where he mentions that 'the singers remain behind a mass constructed of costumes and masks' (ibid, p. 97). The 'truc' appears in the original as a drawing of an eye (cf. chap. 3, n. 26).

19 *Dial*, p. 23. The décor in the score is credited to the composer's painter son Théodore, who worked with Cocteau on these initial designs. But see chap. 1, p. 6 and n. 23.

20 E. Freeman, in the notes to the Blackwell edition of the play (Oxford, 1976), p. 46, n. 3.

21 Quoted in Paul Surer, *Le Théâtre français contemporain* (Paris: Société d'Édition et d'Enseignement Supérieur, 1964), p. 29.

22 Pitoëff had also performed the Devil's Dance in the original Lausanne production

of *The Soldier's Tale* in 1918. In the first production of *Orphée* he played the title
role opposite his wife Ludmilla.

23 *Dial*, p. 23.
24 See the preface to the published score.
25 Ibid.
26 The much-trumpeted revival of *The Rite of Spring* in December 1920 was followed
in 1922 by the premières of *Renard* (1916) and *Mavra* (1921–2), and in 1923 by that
of *Les Noces* (essentially 1914–17). The Paris première of *The Soldier's Tale* (1918)
was in 1924.
27 See Bibliography. There is no piano in the *Octet*, but an early sketch of it survives
in the lay-out of a miniature piano concerto.
28 Lourié, 'Oedipus Rex' (1927), p. 248.

3 In which the music unfolds

1 'Some ideas about my Octuor', in White, *Stravinsky*, pp. 574–7.
2 Lourié, 'La Sonate pour piano de Strawinsky', p. 100.
3 Lourié, 'Neogothic and neoclassic', p. 8.
4 See chap. 1, n. 1.
5 Compare Lourié, 'Neogothic and neoclassic', p. 4: 'seeking to construct neoclassical
forms by triumphing over personal utterance and affirming as the basis of an
objective style a greater-than-individualistic principle'. The original printing of
'Some ideas about my Octuor' carried a short editorial preface (not reproduced by
White though clearly prompted by the composer), which contains the significant
remark: 'Free from all the Russian influence that is felt in most of his work, the
Octuor marks the most advanced point that Stravinsky has attained in music' (*The
Arts*, Brooklyn, 1924, p. 5). The implication that Russianism was retrogressive is
clear.
6 White, *Stravinsky*, p. 574.
7 Ibid, p. 576.
8 See Andriessen and Schönberger, *The Apollonian Clockwork*, pp. 18–20, for a more
detailed, if still over-simplified, discussion of the relationship between Stravinsky
and Magritte.
9 *Chron*, p. 204. The Serenade was completed on 9 October 1925, 'but at least five
years earlier than that I had been aware of the need to compose a large-scale dramatic
work' (*Dial*, p. 21).
10 Lourié, 'Oedipus-Rex' (1927).
11 *Chron*, pp. 215–16.
12 Lourié, 'Oedipus-Rex', p. 240.
13 *Dial*, p. 22.
14 Ibid, p. 25.
15 Ibid, p. 27.
16 It is worth comparing the role of Stravinsky's Speaker with that of the narrator in
Honegger's earlier dramatic oratorio *Le Roi David* (1921). Though Honegger uses

his narrator to articulate a series of sharply drawn tableaux, there is never anything oblique or ironic about the treatment. The speaking voice is simply used (in the rhetorical French manner) to carry the story along swiftly, but in straightforward narrative fashion, as in a film. Honegger, incidentally, wrote the music for the 1921 production of Cocteau's *Antigone*, and later (1927) turned the text of the play into an opera, apparently in ignorance of the *Oedipus* project, and certainly in ignorance of its nature.

17 Not so designated in the score.

18 'Oedipus-Rex', p. 244.

19 'Tonality without fifths: remarks on the first movement of Stravinsky's Concerto for piano and wind instruments', *In Theory Only*, 2 (1977), pp. 53–70.

20 See *Dial*, p. 27, and Bernstein, *The Unanswered Question* (Cambridge, Mass: Harvard University Press, 1976), quoted in *SPD*, p. 270.

21 They are analysed in painstaking detail by Pierre Boulez in 'Stravinsky demeure', translated by the present author as 'Stravinsky remains', in *Stocktakings from an Apprenticeship* (Oxford University Press: Oxford, 1991), pp. 55–110.

22 Lourié, 'Oedipus Rex', pp. 241, 246–7.

23 Ibid, p. 244.

24 For some reason, the chorus sings 'Vale' ('Farewell') instead of 'Ave' ('Hail'). See *Dial*, p. 31, for Stravinsky's notes on this and other errors in the Latin text.

25 Throughout this book I have adopted Stravinsky's spelling, which substitutes 'k' for 'c' to ensure a hard articulation in front of soft vowels (necessary particularly for French singers). 'Miki' is a slightly different case. The Latin word is 'mihi', which in Russian is transliterated as 'михи', where the 'x' sounds like the 'ch' in 'loch'. Stravinsky includes this in his list of spelling mistakes. But he may well have preferred 'k' at the time because a French singer would voice 'h' even less than an English or German one, whereas some articulation is essential with the dotted rhythm in 'Non reperias'. There is no equivalent to the Russian 'x' in French.

26 Degrees of seeing make up a symbolic sub-plot in Sophocles's play. Sight and insight, eyes and vision, form a thread of metaphor, culminating, of course, in Oedipus's self-blinding at the moment of clearest seeing. Presumably Cocteau's 'truc' with the drawing of an eye, in his letter of January 1926, refers in some way to this idea. See chap. 2, n. 18.

27 Oedipus's long tied semibreve before the double bar at fig. 83 was added in the revision of 1948. In the 1927 score Tiresias's D ends pat at the double bar and Oedipus enters immediately after it.

28 The single exception is the adaptation of the 'Creavistis' music to the words 'Eg' Oedipus clarus, ego', just before the end. The connection is obvious, of course, but does not support the general point made here.

29 Or would be, if Stravinsky had not cut out these particular three words. In his 1951 recording with Cocteau, on the other hand, the words 'il a peur' are retained (as they are in the 1952 and 1959 live performances perpetuated on disc) but the chorus reprise is not. But this may have been an editing decision. Cocteau dubbed the narration some months after the music was recorded, and Stravinsky may well not

have troubled to record the chorus twice. See Philip Stuart, *Igor Stravinsky – The Composer in the Recording Studio*, for the relevant discographic details. This question is discussed further in chap. 4.

30 'Avertissement', in White, *Stravinsky*, pp. 577–8.

31 *SPD*, p. 270.

32 In *Dial*, pp. 22–3, Stravinsky draws a distinction between 'music drama' or 'prose opera' (Wagner, Schoenberg's *Erwartung*) and 'opera' or 'verse opera' (his own *Rake's Progress*). It is clear that Verdi, too, was a composer of verse operas. Realism in his work is subject to rigid conventions which translate it into a virtual quality, accepted as such by composer, performers and audience alike. By contrast, Wagner's realism masquerades as 'really real': asks us, as the saying goes, to suspend our disbelief and accept his world of fat sopranos, middle-aged boys, and sensuous harmony as ordinary in the sense that the modern popular cinema invites us to accept its images as ordinary. But it needs emphasising (and Stravinsky himself hints) that these distinctions are to some extent polemical, and much less clearcut than argument tries to make them.

33 Nevertheless the much-quoted diminished seventh arpeggios at the words 'clamare' and 'ululare' are a Bachian as much as Verdian image. See, for instance, the many occurrences in the *St Matthew Passion* at moments of anguish, perplexity or menace, such as Peter's 'weinete bitterlich' or the choral shouts of 'Barabbas'.

34 In the opera the Shepherd is never referred to directly by the Speaker, except as the 'witness', a reference Stravinsky left out of his 1962 recording, rightly considering it obscure. But in the Latin text of this scene the Shepherd is identified only as the Messenger's accomplice in rescuing Oedipus, never as the escaped witness of Laius's murder (though Oedipus has just made the connection, for those with good Latin, x-ray hearing and lightning responses, in his duet with Jocasta). Strictly speaking the two separate characters (Shepherd and Messenger) are not called for dramatically unless this link is explicit. But Stravinsky needed both a tenor and a bass-baritone soloist, and this is probably why the two roles were retained.

35 As noted in chap. 2 (p. 20) Oedipus's exit is supposed to be carried out 'on the spot and by means of a trapdoor'. But in *Dial* (pp. 23–4), Stravinsky seems to advocate re-masking Oedipus, 'behind his individual curtain or in the dark', without his actually moving at all. The change may simply be in reaction to the 'ideas' of unsympathetic stage directors. But it may equally reflect an original difference in conception between Stravinsky and the Cocteau of *Orphée*.

36 'Stravinsky's Oedipus as 20th-century hero'; see Bibliography.

37 *Dial*, p. 29.

38 See n. 19 above, with particular reference to his tendency to leave out the fifth degree of the primary triad.

39 As before, a reading of Sophocles is essential for a piece-by-piece revelation of the complete picture. But the opera text is itself in general terms reasonably unambiguous at this stage.

40 See fig. 117. The rhythm goes back to Jocasta's 'Nonn' erubeskite', and is several

times anticipated by Oedipus in the first act. But it only acquires symbolic force in connection with the word 'trivium'.

41 *Dial*, p. 30.

42 Not that he was any less rude about the fanfares, 'which remind me of the now badly tarnished trumpets of early 20th-Century-Fox'. *Dial*, p. 30.

43 To be exact, it survives in the first (or play) version of Cocteau's text, but not in the opera libretto.

44 See van den Toorn, *The Music of Igor Stravinsky*, for an exhaustive treatment of this subject.

45 Compare, for instance, the melodic contour of the 'Figlio del cielo' incantation with that of 'Divum Jocastae caput mortuum'; the up-rushing string figure of 'Si! Rinasce!' with that of Stravinsky's accompaniment; and the harmony of the two passages, purely octatonic in Stravinsky, nearly so in Puccini. Even the treatment of the chorus in the two works has similarities.

46 *Dial*, p. 29.

4 How it all came to be known

1 *Poet*, pp. 55–6.

2 Ibid, p. 53.

3 *SSCI*, p. 95, n. 39.

4 Thoroughgoing consideration of such matters is beyond the scope of the present study, and must in any case await a systematic comparison of the two main manuscript sources: the complete sketchbook in the Paul Sacher Stiftung in Basel, and the draft vocal score in the Library of Congress, Washington DC. The Washington score is the one listed by White as 'the manuscript vocal score' (*Stravinsky*, p. 327). But the disordered character of its opening pages suggests that it started life as a working draft, whose order of composition and degree of reworking reflect those of the Basel sketchbook and are broadly as described in the text here. Only after composing the first scene did Stravinsky cue the disordered sections one to the next and thereafter treat the draft score as an increasingly tidy vocal score. Perhaps this supports my speculation about the first scene text. But the evidence is conflicting. As early as 8 January, Cocteau had written to Daniélou that 'I await – we await – your first text with the greatest impatience'. See Steegmuller, *Cocteau*, p. 358. But by that time Stravinsky had already sketched part of the first chorus.

5 Tappolet, *Correspondance Ansermet-Strawinsky*, vol. 2, p. 133; translation by the present writer.

6 Not counting *Pulcinella*, whose orchestra is in any case small and not quite standard (it lacks clarinets) and whose music is, in broad terms, an arrangement.

7 Klemperer's memory that the accompaniment was played four-hands by Stravinsky and Prokofiev seems to be at fault. See chap. 1, n. 33.

8 See, for instance, his letter to his mother, cited in n. 3 above.

9 *Dial*, p. 25.

10 Heyworth, *Conversations with Klemperer*, p. 60.
11 Henri Malherbe in *Le Temps*, 8 June 1927. A note in Stravinsky's own *Oedipus* file, now in Basel, records that the choir was 'on the stage in front of the curtain, with the singers [chanteurs] in the orchestra'. No doubt purely practical considerations dictated this curious arrangement.
12 See his long and intelligent review in the *Nouvelle Revue Française*, 29 (1927), pp. 244–8. 'One has but a single desire: that he shut up at the earliest possible moment, this pretentiously-named puppeteer.'
13 *Dearest Bubushkin*, p. 36, n. 7.
14 Ibid, p. 38. See also Herbert Antcliffe's review in *The Musical Times*, 69 (June 1928), p. 555.
15 Not apparently Lothar Wallenstein, as given in Schouvalov and Borovsky, *Stravinsky on Stage*, p. 130, nor Schalk's assistant Robert Heger, as stated in Stanley Sadie (ed.), *The New Grove Dictionary of Music and Musicians*, vol. 19 (Macmillan: London, 1980), p. 727. Schalk is credited both by the *Neue Musik Zeitung*, 49 (1928), p. 437, and by *The Musical Times*, 69 (April 1928), pp. 367–8. On the same bill, Schalk conducted Alfano's opera *Madonna Imperia*.
16 *Zeitschrift für Musik*, 95 (April 1928), pp. 218–19.
17 In *Dial*, p. 25, he calls the Berlin run 'the first staged performances'. But Craft reports that a friend had described Alfred Roller's Vienna designs to the composer as 'a mélange of Louis-Quinze and Hubert Robert'. *SSCIII*, p. 519.
18 The design (including a ground-plan) is reproduced in Schouvalov and Borovsky, *Stravinsky on Stage*, pp. 128-9, and (without the plan) in Heyworth, *Otto Klemperer*, vol. 1, p. 265. Dülberg designed *Oedipus Rex* again for the Teatro Colon in Buenos Aires in August 1931. In *Dial* (p. 25), Stravinsky wrote: 'I wince when I recall the [Kroll] performances'. But according to Craft, Stravinsky considered Dülberg's design 'a perfect realization, the decorative sobriety and sensitive positioning of the soloists and chorus resulting in a performance that was a logical extension of my score'. *SSCIII*, p. 519.
19 *Dial*, p. 25; *Zeitschrift für Musik*, 95 (April 1928), pp. 216–17. Adorno, who attended the dress rehearsal, had expected a 'man to come on suddenly in a *Frack* and dance a charleston', but heard only later that 'a *Frack* really was specified and had been quite wrongly exchanged for a "timeless costume"'. One wonders whether his quotation of Diesterweg's description means that the change was made between the dress rehearsal and the performance. See *Neue Musik Zeitung*, 49 (1928), pp. 419–20.
20 See Heyworth, *Otto Klemperer*, vol. 1, pp. 264–5; *Dial*, p. 25; *Conv*, p. 75. Despite the presumed conservative character of such an audience, Heinrich Strobel reported (*Neue Musik Zeitung*, 49 (1928), p. 437) that the applause was vigorous. But Schoenberg's reaction was hostile (see *Style and Idea*, pp. 482–3). His remarks are dated 24 February. Did he therefore, like Adorno, attend the dress rehearsal? According to Heyworth (p. 266, note), the revival of the opera in May had the Speaker in a dark suit.
21 A photograph of the Düsseldorf production is in *Neue Musik Zeitung*, 49 (1928)

facing p. 536. It seems to show the final scene, with Oedipus blinded, Jocasta still on-stage behind him, and the chorus averting their gaze. Creon is also on-stage with the Messenger (so these roles were not doubled). But the detail is not completely clear.

22 I rely here on Schouvalov and Borovsky, *Stravinsky on Stage*, p. 133, though the listing there is both somewhat provisional and, at times, inaccurate or incomplete. It does not mention, for instance, the Soviet stage première, at Yerevan, Armenia, in 1963.

23 This was the British public première, conducted by Ansermet. Stravinsky had himself conducted two broadcast performances for the BBC, on 12 and 13 May 1928. But his memory of having conducted it for the BBC in June 1927 seems to be at fault (see *Chron*, p. 217). Vera's diary (*Dearest Bubushkin*, p. 36) mentions his broadcast concert on the 19th, but does not give the programme. Reviews of the 1928 broadcasts clearly imply (though without stating) that they were the first. Britten's enthusiastic review of the 1936 performance is reprinted in *Tempo*, 120 (March 1977), pp. 10–12.

24 *Sunday Times*, 20 May 1928 (Newman); *Daily Telegraph*, 17 September 1927 (Hughes). Hughes mentions Klemperer's projected London performance for the Royal Philharmonic Society in January 1928, but this project collapsed because Klemperer demanded too much rehearsal time. See Heyworth, *Otto Klemperer*, vol. 1, p. 319.

25 *Chron*, p. 228. Stravinsky was admittedly more familiar with the notoriously difficult, factious, claque-ridden world of the Parisian musical theatre.

26 The work had previously been given in concert performance by the Boston Symphony Orchestra under Koussevitsky in Boston on 24 April 1928.

27 Lawrence Gilman, *New York Herald Tribune*, 22 April 1931. See Oja (ed.), *Stravinsky in 'Modern Music'*, p. 34, for a preliminary sketch by Jones of this staging.

28 Olin Downes, *New York Times*, 22 April 1931.

29 *The Mask*, April 1908, quoted in Braun, *The Director and the Stage*, p. 93. By contrast, Ingmar Bergman told Stravinsky in 1961 that he would avoid masks if he staged *Oedipus*: 'A mask may be beautiful, and it can be a useful façade for all sorts of things, but the price, which is the loss of contact, is too great.' See Craft, *The Chronicle of a Friendship*, p. 118.

30 *Dial*, p. 25. He seems not to have seen, however, the Rome production designed by Giacomo Manzù in February 1964; nor did he live to see the Hockney designs for John Dexter's production at the New York Met in December 1981. See Pasler (ed.), *Confronting Stravinsky*, plate 6.3, for a colour photograph of the Dexter staging.

31 *Dial*, p. 25. Stravinsky himself conducted the performance, which is preserved on record: Disques Montaigne (CD) TCE 8760, with an accompanying booklet containing many photographs of the masks and stage settings. For additional description of the tableaux, see Cocteau, *Journal d'un inconnu* (Paris: Bernard Grasset, 1953), pp. 225–30.

32 For the Cologne recording, see below, n. 42. The London performance is also on

record: Fonit-Cetra DOC 11. Cocteau annoyed Stravinsky on this occasion by playing heavily to the gallery. See Paul Horgan, *Encounters with Stravinsky* (New York: Farrar Straus and Giroux, 1972), pp. 163–5. Philip Stuart, *Igor Stravinsky*, is now the source for all discographic information on the composer.

33 Nor it seems the Paris audience, who booed Cocteau. Steegmuller, *Cocteau*, p. 480.

34 *SSCI*, p. 119, n. 63. But Stuart, *Igor Stravinsky*, p. 77, lists a Belgian Radio recording of 29 May in which a Speaker is credited (Georges Genicot). Did Stravinsky conduct the work twice on this visit?

35 *Dial*, p. 29.

36 *SPD*, p. 639, n. 166.

37 Letter of 11 October 1947, *SSCIII*, p. 318.

38 It was only after becoming a US citizen in December 1945 that Stravinsky was in a position to protect his works in this way, so far as their exploitation in the USA was concerned.

39 See the letter to Hawkes referred to in n. 37. But in his index of Stravinsky publications, Dominique-René de Lerma lists the score as published and cites a plate number. See *Igor Fedorovitch Stravinsky: a Practical Guide to Publications of his Music* (Kent, Ohio: Kent State University Press, 1974), pp. 47–8. But de Lerma is not always a reliable or complete source; for instance, he makes no separate entries for orchestral materials, which often carry a different plate number from the full score. In any case the assignment of a plate number is no proof of publication, as the 1920 *Symphonies of wind instruments* shows.

40 *Chronicle of a Friendship*, p. 318.

41 Ibid. The Toronto *Oedipus* under Craft was, as already mentioned, a concert performance. But curiously enough Toronto saw a staged version six months later (by the Opera School of the Royal Conservatory of Music), in which, once again, the chorus was in the pit. Stravinsky might have approved this. But did he sanction the rearrangement of the chorus parts for SATB choir?

42 The 1951 recording was apparently made in Cologne on 8 October. According to Philip Stuart, *Igor Stravinsky*, p. 36, Cocteau recorded the speeches the following May in Paris. Stuart also lists (p. 76) a Bavarian Radio recording of the composer's Munich performance on 21 October in which the narration is delivered in German by Alois Maria Giani. Presumably in Cologne, too, the narration was in German but Philips preferred a French Speaker for the disc. See also chap. 3, n. 29.

43 Craft, *Chronicle of a Friendship*, p. 318.

Appendix B The Latin and its setting

1 'Stravinsky's "Rejoicing Discovery"': see Bibliography. The title was prompted by a remark of Stravinsky's own. See *Expo*, p. 121.

2 No doubt Stravinsky was aware, as Albright assures us, of the quantitative nature of Latin verse, and also of its systematic tendency to play 'natural' accent off against metric accent. But this property is not quite the same as the capricious misaccentuations of folk poetry. I am grateful to Peter Dennis-Jones for his advice

on this and other technical points to do with the Latin language. See also D. Albright, *The Music Box and the Nightingale*, p. 33.

Appendix C Cast and orchestra

1 *Dial*, p. 27.
2 'Some ideas about my Octuor', in White, *Stravinsky*, p. 574.

Select bibliography

Albright, Daniel. *The Music Box and the Nightingale* (New York: Gordon & Breach, 1989)

Andriessen, Louis, and Schönberger, Elmer. *The Apollonian Clockwork*, trans. Jeff Hamburg (Oxford: Oxford University Press, 1989)

Asaf'yev, Boris. *A Book about Stravinsky*, trans. Richard F. French (Ann Arbor: UMI Research Press, 1982)

Benjamin, William E. 'Tonality without fifths: remarks' on the first movement of Stravinsky's Concerto for piano and wind instruments', *In Theory Only*, 2 (1977), pp. 53–70

Boucourechliev, André. *Stravinsky*, trans. Martin Cooper (London: Gollancz, 1987)

Braun, Edward. *The Director and the Stage* (London: Methuen, 1982)

(ed.). *Meyerhold on Theatre* (London: Eyre Methuen, 1969)

Britten, Benjamin. 'Britten on "Oedipus Rex" and "Lady Macbeth"', *Tempo*, 120 (March 1977), pp. 10–12

Buckle, Richard. *Diaghilev* (London: Weidenfeld & Nicolson, 1979)

Cocteau, Jean. *Orphée*, edited with an introduction by E. Freeman (Oxford: Blackwell, 1976)

Œdipe-Roi. Roméo et Juliette (Paris: Librairie Plon, 1928)

Œuvres complètes (Geneva: Marguerat, 1950)

Le Rappel à l'ordre (Paris: Stock, 1926)

Cone, Edward T. 'The uses of convention: Stravinsky and his models', *Musical Quarterly*, 48 (1962), pp. 287–99

Craft, Robert. (*See also* under Igor Stravinsky and Vera Stravinsky.) *Stravinsky: the Chronicle of a Friendship* (London: Gollancz, 1972)

(ed.). *Stravinsky: Selected Correspondence*, 3 vols (London: Faber & Faber, 1982, 1984, 1985)

(ed.). *Dearest Bubushkin: Selected Letters and Diaries of Vera and Igor Stravinsky* (London: Thames & Hudson, 1985)

Drew, David. 'Stravinsky's revisions', *The Score*, 20 (1957), pp. 47–58

Druskin, Mikhail. *Igor Stravinsky: his Personality, Works and Views* (Cambridge: Cambridge University Press, 1983)

Graves, Robert. *The Greek Myths*, vol. 1 (Harmondsworth: Penguin, 1960)

Heyworth, Peter. *Conversations with Klemperer* (London: Gollancz, 1973)

Otto Klemperer: His Life and Times, vol. 1 (Cambridge: Cambridge University Press, 1983), p. 246

Joergensen, Johannes. *Saint François d'Assise*, French translation by Teodor de Wyzewa (Paris: Librairie Académique Perrin, 1910)

Karlinsky, Simon. 'Stravinsky and Russian preliterate theater', in Pasler (1986), pp. 3–15

Lederman, Minna (ed.). *Stravinsky in the Theatre* (New York: Pellegrini & Cudahy, 1949)

Lessem, Alan. 'Schoenberg, Stravinsky and neo-Classicism: the issues reexamined', *Musical Quarterly*, 68 (1982), pp. 527–42

Lesure, François (ed.). *Stravinsky: Études et témoignages* (Paris: Jean-Claude Lattès, 1982)

Lourié, Arthur. 'La Sonate pour piano de Strawinsky', *La Revue musicale*, 6 (1925), pp. 100–14

   'Oedipus Rex', *La Revue musicale*, 8 (1927), pp. 240–53

   'Neogothic and Neoclassic', *Modern Music*, 5 (1928), pp. 3–8

   'A propos de l'*Apollon* d'Igor Strawinsky', *Musique*, 1 (1928), pp. 117–19

Maritain, Jacques. *Art et scolastique* (Paris: L'Art Catholique, 1920)

Mellers, Wilfrid. 'Stravinsky's Oedipus as 20th-century hero', in Paul Henry Lang (ed.), *Stravinsky: A New Appraisal of his Work* (New York: Norton, 1963), pp. 34–46

Messing, Scott. *Neoclassicism in Music: From the Genesis of the Concept through the Schoenberg/Stravinsky Polemic* (Ann Arbor and London: UMI Research Press, 1988)

Oja, Carol J. (ed.). *Stravinsky in 'Modern Music'* (New York: Da Capo Press, 1982)

Pasler, Jann (ed.). *Confronting Stravinsky* (Berkeley, Los Angeles, London: University of California Press, 1986)

Schloezer, Boris de. Review of *Oedipus Rex* in *Nouvelle revue française*, 29 (1927), pp. 244–8

Schoenberg, Arnold. 'Stravinsky's *Oedipus*', in Leonard Stein (ed.), *Style and Idea: Selected Writings of Arnold Schoenberg* (London: Faber & Faber, 1975), pp. 482–3

Schouvalov, Alexander, and Borovsky, Victor. *Stravinsky on Stage* (London: Stainer & Bell, 1982)

Steegmuller, Francis. *Cocteau: a Biography* (London: Macmillan, 1970)

Stravinsky, Igor. 'Une lettre de Stravinsky sur Tchaïkovski', *Le Figaro*, 18 May 1922; reprinted in Lesure (1982), pp. 239–40

   'Some ideas about my Octuor', *The Arts* (Brooklyn, January 1924), pp. 4–6; reprinted in White (1979), pp. 574–7

   'Avertissement', *The Dominant* (December 1927); reprinted with an English translation in White (1979), pp. 577–8.

   Chroniques de ma vie (Paris: Denoël & Steele, 1935–6); anon. English translation as *Chronicle of my Life* (London: Gollancz, 1936)

   Poétique musicale (Cambridge, Mass.: Harvard University Press, 1942); trans. Arthur Knodel and Ingolf Dahl as *Poetics of Music* (Harvard, 1947)

Stravinsky, Igor, and Craft, Robert. *Conversations with Igor Stravinsky* (London: Faber & Faber, 1959)

   Expositions and Developments (London: Faber & Faber, 1962)

   Dialogues and a Diary (London: Faber & Faber, 1968); reissued without the diary section as *Dialogues* (1982)

Stravinsky, Vera, and Craft, Robert. *Stravinsky in Pictures and Documents* (New York: Simon & Schuster, 1978)

Stuart, Philip. *Igor Stravinsky – The Composer in the Recording Studio* (New York, Westport and London: Greenwood Press, 1991)

Tappolet, Claude (ed.). *Correspondance Ansermet–Strawinsky* (1914–67), vol. 2 (Geneva: Georg, 1991)

Taruskin, Richard. 'Stravinsky's "rejoicing discovery" and what it meant: in defense of his notorious text setting', in Ethan Haimo and Paul Johnson (eds), *Stravinsky Retrospectives* (Lincoln and London: University of Nebraska Press, 1987), pp. 162–99

van den Toorn, Pieter C. *The Music of Igor Stravinsky* (New Haven and London: Yale University Press, 1983)

Vlad, Roman. *Stravinsky*, 2nd edn (Oxford: Oxford University Press, 1967)

Walsh, Stephen. *The Music of Stravinsky*, new edn (Oxford: Oxford University Press, 1993)

White, Eric Walter. *Stravinsky: the Composer and his Works*, 2nd edn (London: Faber & Faber, 1979)

Index